Revelation 12:3-4, NIV:
³Then another sign appeared with seven heads and ten horns and seven crowns on his heads.
⁴ His *tail* swept a third of the stars out of the sky and flung them to the earth.

The TAIL of the dragon is

The Many False Prophets

Isaiah 9:15, NIV:
The elders and prominent men are the head, *the prophets who teach lies are the tail.*

By Donald A. Peart

Copyright © 2001
Donald A. Peart

ISBN: 0-9702301-2-5

Library of Congress Control Number: 2003090728

Printed in the United States by:
Morris Publishing
3212 East Highway 30
Kearney, NE 68847
1-800-650-7888

Acknowledgement

The Lord Jesus is preeminent in everything. All that is accomplished through His Church is a direct result of His Grace. He is the living God. The real, live flesh and bone Jesus is at the right hand of the Father interceding for us. We are not serving dumb logs and stones. Therefore, because He is the living God, He communicates to us. Therefore, I give tribute first to the Spirit of the living Son who is still speaking in us.

Special thanks to my beautiful wife Judith and the five children the Lord gave us. Judith and children I appreciate the liberty to write because of your understanding the will of the Lord.

Thanks to **The Shepherd's Tent** family for supplying their measure. We are laborers together in the work of our Lord Jesus Christ. It is my prayer that great grace continues to be upon **The Shepherd's Tent** family.

Table of Contents

Preface

Poem

Preface

I greet you, in the name of our Lord Jesus Christ. The Spirit of the Lord has directed me to write concerning the false prophet—a spirit. This directive came in the mid 1990s. He said, "Send it to the seven Churches sown across the land." The Lord instructed me to "prophesy against the false prophet, and <u>cast</u> him down." I am to "speak **TO** his (the false prophet's) purposes, and prophesy his demise." This command was executed in Volume I *The False Prophet, Alias, Another Beast*, and followed by Volume II, *Then the angel said to me: "Why are you astonished? I will explain to you the mystery of.... the beast..."*

I have, therefore, set forth in order this synoptic book in keeping with the series. The book is brief for many reasons. One of the reasons is that most of the youth of today do not have the patience to read extensive writings. Therefore, this is catering to their need that they might have an understanding about the many false prophets. However, for the person who enjoys serious study, there are many references. These references will assist the serious students, and broaden his or her understanding.

It is also my desire that all readers read the entire series—Volume I, *The False Prophet, Alias, Another Beast;* Volume II *The Beast* and this volume—for an accurate understanding of the spirit of the false prophet and the beast associated with the false prophet. This is because some of the teachings of the series were hidden from other generations; however, the Holy Spirit is now revealing these mysteries to His apostles and prophets.

I pray that the first four chapters may be enlightening to you, strengthening your resistance against the many false prophets, by the anointing in you. Finally, I also pray that the fifth chapter encourage you to receive the true apostolic and prophetic ministries.

Donald A. Peart

The Shepherd's Tent

CHAPTER 1
TWO HORNS <u>LIKE</u> A LAMB

Revelation 13:11, NIV:
*Then I saw another beast, coming out of the earth. He had **two horns like a lamb,** but he **spoke** like a dragon.*

I John 4:1, NIV:
*Dear friends, do not believe every spirit, but test the spirits to see whether they are from God, because **many false prophets** have gone out into the world.*

One of the challenges of this age, as disciples, will be to know the many false prophets who are among us, **and** with that knowledge still function in the Spirit and in the love of God among them (Genesis 41; Daniel 2; Exodus 7; John 6:70-71). Before I site some examples of how to function among the false ones, I will show you how they dress.

False prophets like to wear *"sheep's clothing."* The quotes above gave some explicit description concerning an entity called *"another beast"* (Revelation 13:11), alias, *"the false prophet"* (Revelation 16:13; Revelation 20:10). This being is called a *"beast."* However, this same beast has *"two horns like a lamb."* Do not stop there, he also speaks *"like a dragon."* This description beloved is deception at work. In every generation, there are entities that have horns **like** *"a lamb"*—Jesus. Yet, they speak **like** *"a dragon"*—Satan (Revelation 12:9). According to the verse above, having horns like a lamb does not make a person speak like a sheep (Isaiah 53:7; I Peter 2:21-23). [Horns are part of the clothing of a male sheep (a ram)]. It is the **words** from **within** that are spoken which determine the nature of that person. Allow me to explain.

SHEEP'S CLOTHING

Matthew 7:15, NIV:
Watch out for false prophets. They come to you in **sheep's clothing,** *but inwardly they are ferocious wolves.*

Listen to Jesus. He said false prophets would come in *"sheep's clothing."* He did **not** say, "They would come as sheep." False prophets are not sheep of Jesus. They can only dress **as** a sheep. "Clothing" means just that "clothing." If you take a wolf and clothed the wolf with some lamb's skin, there is still a wolf under that lamb's skin. Do you understand? Jesus in His wisdom knew this. Therefore, He said false prophets will come in sheep's clothing. However, underneath the sheep's clothing are *"ferocious wolves."* This compliments Revelation 13:11.

The beast that *"spoke like a dragon"* also *"had two horns like a lamb."* This lizard, dragon, was dressed in sheep's clothing. He was clothed with lamb's horns. However, internally he is still a dragon. Do you see it

2

now? The point is this: Christians must be able to see the heart, like God, and not concentrate on outward appearance. Hear the word to Samuel concerning choosing leaders—*"Do not consider his appearance or his height, for I have rejected him. The LORD **does not** look at the things man looks at. Man looks at the outward appearance, **but the LORD looks at the heart"*** (I Samuel 16:7).

HE JUDGES.... THE HEART

Hebrews 4:12, NIV:
*For the **word of God** is living and active. Sharper than any double-edged sword, it penetrates even to dividing soul and spirit, joints and marrow; **it judges the thoughts and attitudes of the heart.***

How will the disciples know those not approved by God? The Text above says *"the word of God.... judges the thoughts and attitudes of the heart."* But Brother Peart, what is the application of the statement you made? The verse said the word of God *"penetrates."* In the next verse it says, *"Nothing in all creation is hidden from **God's sight**. Everything is uncovered and laid bare before the eyes of him to whom we must give account"* (Hebrews 4:13). This verse, which is a continuation of verse twelve, calls *"the word of God" 'God's sight.'*

Therefore, the word of God is the eyes of God. Do you see this? I will now make a simple statement that may revolutionize your life. If the Word of God is the

3

sight of God—and it is, consequently, if His disciples put the Word of God in their heart, then, His disciples also through the Word *"penetrates even to dividing soul and spirit, joints and marrow; it judges the thoughts and attitudes of the heart."* Yes! Yes! Yes! This knowledge beloved should encourage you to study and muse on the word of God. God's Word *"penetrates."* His Word is so sharp and keen it *"judges the thoughts," "attitude of the heart"* and it is *"dividing soul and spirit."* This brings me to my next points. We must use the Word of God to see the **spirit** of the false ones (I John 4:1). In Jesus' term we must *"watch for false prophets ... inwardly"* (Matthew 7:15). This is the command on how to judge false prophets. They may have sheep's clothing of lamb's horn, power. However, their spirit may be unclean; dragon-like and/or frog-like (Revelation 13:11; 16:13).

DO NOT BELIEVE EVERY SPIRIT

I John 4:1, NIV:
Dear friends, do not believe every spirit, but test the spirits to see whether they are from God, because many false prophets have gone out into the world.

The command by the same man of God, John the beloved, who saw the beast in Revelation 13:11 is: *"do not believe every spirit."* He said we should *"test the spirits."* John did not stop there. He linked *"the spirits"* to *"many false prophets."* How did John do this? He did it by using the conjunction *"because."* This is

4

important to know. Let us look at the verse above with all that was said in the previous paragraphs. Remember what Jesus said to the disciples? He said, *"Watch out for false prophets. They come to you in sheep's clothing, but* **inwardly** *they are ferocious wolves"* (Matthew 7:15).

Jesus said the way to know false ones is to understand that *"inwardly"* they are wolves. I said above, "a person may clothes a wolf with sheep's clothing, but there is still a wolf under the clothes." I learned that form Jesus' statement in Matthews 7:15. The false prophets may look like sheep, however, *"inwardly"* **their spirit**—they are really wolves, or dragons.

Let us compare everything together (I Corinthians 2:13). In Revelation 13: 11 John said that "another beast" had two horns like a lamb. However, *"he spoke like a dragon."* Our Lord said, *"The good man brings good things out of the good stored up in his heart, and the evil man brings evil things out of the evil stored up in his heart.* ***For out of the overflow of his heart his mouth speaks"*** (Luke 6:45). The beast may have lamb's horn, but, his **mouth** told on him. He spoke like a dragon ***"out of the overflow of his heart."*** Jesus said the *"mouth"* reveals the *"good"* or *"evil"* that is in the *"heart"* as one *"speaks."*

Thus, this beast that looked like a lamb outwardly is really a dragon *"inwardly"*—heart and/or spirit. John called this inward part *"spirit."* Therefore, John said do not believe every spirit. We are to *"test the spirit."* How do we test? The Word of God, which is the eyes of God, as we learned earlier, divides *"soul and* **spirit.*** There is also another important **person** involved in seeing/exposing the antichrist spirits.

I Corinthians 12:7, NIV:
*Now to each one the manifestation of the **Spirit** is given for the **common good**... to another **distinguishing between spirits**.*

The person of the Holy Spirit also extends a *"service"* (I Corinthians 12:5) of distinguishing between spirits. This beloved is the love of God for His Church. He has given us His Holy Spirit to distinguish between spirits *"for the common good."* He always wants **good** for us, not evil. Therefore, He will expose all that will not do us *"good."* He is the **Holy** (Greek: Hagios also means **Clean**) Spirit. Therefore, He knows all the dirty (unclean spirits) (Revelation 16:13-14). Now take note: there are nine gifts of the Spirit listed in I Corinthians 12:8-11and there are nine fruit of the Spirit listed in Galatians 5.

The fruit of the Spirit that lines up with the gift of *"distinguishing between spirits"* is the fruit of *"faith."* The fruit of faith is seventh in line of the nine facets of the fruit of the Spirit and, the gift of distinguishing between spirits is also seventh in line of the gifts listed in I Corinthians 12:8-11. The point is this: As the Clean Spirit of God distinguish between spirits, you must have the fruit of faith working. Because some of the spirits he will show you in people will be so unexpected that you will need the fruit of faith to believe it. In other words, there are false brethren, false prophets, false apostles, false pastors, etc. who claim to be of Christ but they have a spirit which is not of God. Do you understand? If not read the above again. John also made another statement concerning **recognition and/or distinguishing** of the Clean Spirit and the wrong spirit. He said:

I John 4:2-3, NIV:
*²This is how you can recognize the Spirit of God: Every spirit that **acknowledges** that Jesus Christ has come in the flesh is from God, ³but every spirit that **does not acknowledge** Jesus is not from God. This is **the spirit of the antichrist,** which you have heard is coming and even now is already in the world.*

The word *"acknowledges,"* in the Greek means, *"to say the same thing."* In the context of this verse, *"acknowledges"* means the spirits of the prophets must *"say the same thing"* their *"outward appearance"* is saying about Jesus coming in the flesh. In other words, everyone who **says** they believe that *"Jesus Christ has come in the flesh"* is not necessarily a disciple if their spirit is not clean.

James 2:19 said, *"You believe that there is one God. Good! Even the **demons believe** that—and shudder."* Demons believe, so belief alone is not enough. The **spirit** must also confess what the mouth is saying. Paul **served** the Lord with his spirit.

7

Romans 1:9, NIV:
*God, whom I serve with **my whole heart (lit.; my spirit)** in preaching the gospel of his Son, is my witness how constantly I remember you ...*

Romans 1:9, KJV:
*For God is my witness, whom I serve with **my spirit** in the gospel of his Son, that without ceasing I make mention of you always in my prayers ...*

Romans 1:9, NASU:
*For God, whom I serve in **my spirit** in the preaching of the gospel of His Son, is my witness as to how unceasingly I make mention of you ...*

Paul's **spirit** served the Lord along with his *"outward"* confession of his mouth. That is, a person's mouth and/or those who act religious (they have the religious vocabulary, religious dance, religious look, etc) should not be saying he/she believes, yet the spirit in them is serving someone else. Or he/she has an unclean demon acting like they are Disciples of Christ. The Church must realize that there is a real *"spirit of antichrist."*

If a prophet does not have the Spirit of God, he has the spirit of antichrist. Do you see this? We must not believe every spirit. Jesus said words are spirit (John 6:63). The beast in Revelation 13:11 *"spoke like a dragon."* This means out of his mouth precedes a spirit from within. John brought this out in Revelation.

8

Revelation 16:12-14

*[12] The sixth angel poured out his bowl on the great river Euphrates, and its water was dried up to prepare the way for the kings from the East. [13] Then I saw three **evil spirits** that looked like frogs; they came out of the mouth of the dragon, out of the mouth of the beast and out of the **mouth** of the false prophet. [14]They are spirits of demons performing miraculous signs, and they go out to the kings of the whole world, to gather them for the battle on the great day of God Almighty.*

In the verses above John said, *"I saw three **evil spirits** that looked like frogs; they came out of ... the **mouth** of the false prophet."* I John 4:1 says do not believe **every spirit**. He then called the "spirit" *"many false prophets."* In Revelation 16:13, the same thing is said another way. The false prophet had an *"evil (Greek; unclean) spirit"* come out of his mouth.

The false prophet is a spirit and a spirit came out of his mouth, just as, the dragon is a spirit and a spirit came out of his mouth. This one spirit, the false prophet, controls the *"many false prophets."* There is more. The spirit from the false prophet performs *"miraculous signs."* This is part of the sheep's clothing. Allow me to explain.

The clothing of a sheep, including the male sheep, is their **wool** and their **horns.** The wool or sheepskin is for covering (Hebrews 11:37). Who is covering you, **fake** five-fold ministries/priesthood (Joshua 10:3), or the five grace gifts apportioned by Christ (Ephesians 4:7-

11)? One of the many symbols of the horn is power and authority.

Deuteronomy 33:17, NIV:
*In majesty he is like a firstborn bull; his **horns** are the horns of a wild ox. **With them he will gore the nations,** even those at the ends of the earth. Such are the ten thousands of Ephraim; such are the thousands of Manasseh.*

Daniel 8:5-8, NIV:
*[5] As I was thinking about this, suddenly a goat with a prominent **horn** between his eyes came from the west, crossing the whole earth without touching the ground. [6] He came toward the **two-horned** ram I had seen standing beside the canal and charged at him in great rage. [7] I saw **him attack the ram furiously, striking the ram and shattering his two horns.** The ram was powerless to stand against him; the goat knocked him to the ground and trampled on him, and none could rescue the ram from his power.*

The authority of a male goat or, a ram is gained by the use of the power or strength of his horn (Daniel 8). He uses it to fight for leadership within the flock. In fact in Deuteronomy 33:17, the word *"gore"* means to **"but with horns"**, "to war against" (Strong's). The true Lamb of God has seven horns. "Seven," in the Hebrew language, means "complete" and "oath." Therefore, the Lamb of God Jesus has complete or all power and authority (Matthew 28:17) that was established by the oath (Hebrews 6:17). How did He do this?

Jesus "butted" the Devil with His *"seven horns."* The prince of this world **is** *judged* (John 16:11)! My point is this: horns are symbols of power. Thus, the two horns of the false prophet are representative of the miraculous power that it flows in. These lying signs (II Thessalonians 2:9-11) are part of the false prophet's clothing. His clothing of the miraculous is his strength of persuasion (Revelation 13:18). I would like to give a word of balance at this point. The statement above is not saying that all miracles are not of God. God performs miracles (Acts 3:1-8; Acts 5; Acts 11:28, Acts 13: 8-12; Acts 14:6-11; Hebrews 2:4). And on the other hand, John the Baptist—the Elijah Ministry—did no miracle (John 10:41).

HORNS OF POWER

Revelation 5:6, NIV:
Then I saw a Lamb, looking as if it had been slain, standing in the center of the throne, encircled by the four living creatures and the elders. He had **seven horns** *and seven eyes,* **which are the seven spirits of God** *sent out into all the earth.*

Now note: The *"seven horns... are the seven spirits of God"*—**(1) The Spirit of the Lord, (2) the Spirit of Wisdom, (3) the Spirit of Understanding, (4) the Spirit of Counsel, (5) the Spirit of Power, (6) the Spirit of Knowledge and (7) the Spirit of the fear of**

11

the Lord (Study Isaiah 11:2). There are not seven Holy Spirits (Ephesians 4:3-6). However, there are seven manifestations of His Spirit, which means the Holy Spirit has no measure or limit (John 3:34; Revelation 1:4; 3:1, 4:5; 5:6).

In Revelation 13:11, the false prophet also had two horns. These two horns also mean that he operated through two manifestations of lying spirit. One manifestation is: the spirit of antichrist—worshiping images "instead of" Christ (Revelation 13:15), and the other is: the evil frog-like spirit that worked unclean *"miraculous signs"* (Revelation 16:12-14). You must be careful what kind of *"horns"* are performing the miracles you see. Are the miracles from God gathering you to the Lamb of God?

Or, are the signs from the spirit of antichrist gathering you into the *"place"* called *"Armageddon"*— mountain of the gathering or crowd (Revelation 14-16)? Be careful who you are *"gathering"* to and the *"crowd"* that you partake of. There may be spirits of devils leading the gathering into Armageddon (I Timothy 4:1-2 with Revelation 16:13-16). You must test every spirit. The Spirit of *Jesus Christ* (Philippians 1:19) will bring salvation. The spirit of *antichrist* causes a person to leave God and follow the bad crowd (I John 4:6).

WHO IS THE ANTICHRIST?

I John 4:1-3, NIV:
*[1]Dear friends, do not believe **every spirit,** but test the spirits to see whether they are from God, **because many***

false prophets have gone out into the world. *²This is how you can recognize the Spirit of God: Every spirit that acknowledges that Jesus Christ has come in the flesh is from God, ³but every spirit that does not acknowledge Jesus is not from God.* **This is the spirit of the antichrist,** *which you have heard is coming and even now is already in the world.*

I John 2:18-19, NIV:
¹⁸ Dear children, this is the last hour; and as you have heard that the antichrist is coming, even now many antichrists have come. This is how we know it is the last hour. ¹⁹ **They went out from us,** *but they did not really belong to us. For if they had belonged to us, they would have remained with us; but their going showed that none of them belonged to us.*

For many generations, after the death of the first apostles, men have taught that the antichrist is the beast to come. This trend began in the 1500s. However, what they have overlooked is that in every age antichrist exists. The only facets of antichrist **are not** *"the beast"* of Revelation 13:2 or the *"man of lawlessness"* in II Thessalonians 2:3, NIV. **The antichrist is the "many false prophets" AND those who turn back from following Christ Jesus.** Let us examine this truth.

John said believe not every spirit. He then called the *"every spirit"* *"many false prophets."* He did not stop there. The spirit of the false prophets is also called "the spirit of antichrist." They may look **like** Christ. But, do not be deceived. They are *"antichrist"*—"anti" means "instead of, in place of, or against." Do you see this? Antichrist is any false prophet dressed like he is a sheep of Jesus. His/Her purpose is to seduce the saints from following **The Lord Jesus Christ, the Son of God.** How will he/she do this? By false prophesies, false sign, and false miracles. Thus, the seduced also become antichrist (I John 2:19).

I John 4:3, NIV:
But every spirit that does not acknowledge Jesus is not from God. This is the spirit of the **antichrist,** *which you have heard is coming and* **even now is already in the world.**

An important point is this: "the antichrist... **even now** is already in the world." *"For the secret power of lawlessness* **is already at work;** *but the one who now holds it back will continue to do so till he is taken out of the way"* (II Thessalonians 2:7). *"Dear children, this is the last hour; and as you have heard that the antichrist is coming,* **even now** *many antichrists have come. This is how we know it is the last hour"* (I John 2:18). These verses explicitly state that the antichrist is not totally futuristic.

The antichrist exists *"even now."* For emphasis, the antichrist is a spirit that *"is already at work."* Therefore, stop looking for the antichrist to come. It/he/she/they are already here, as we will see in a moment. The next point is this. According to I John the antichrist is a spirit that speaks through false prophets (I John 4:1). In other words, the antichrist is the *"many*

14

false prophets." This point will be developed later in this book. There is also another facet of the antichrist that is serious. **Antichrist is any person who stops following the Christ.**

I John 2:18-19, NIV:
[18] *Dear children, this is the last hour; and as you have heard that the antichrist is coming, even now many antichrists have come. This is how we know it is the last hour.* [19] ***They went out from us,*** *but they did not really belong to us. For if they had belonged to us, they would have remained with us; but their going showed that none of them belonged to us.*

Antichrists are those who ***"went out from us."*** This knowledge should stop people from so easily going back on God. Those who have **not** endured and *"remained with us"* are antichrist. The heavy part about this is that *"they did not really belong to us."* Anyone who denies Christ after knowing Him is an antichrist. That is why they did not really belong to us. The Bible calls them liars. Their actions lie and say that Jesus is not the Christ when they turn their back on him.

"Who is the liar? It is the man who denies (or contradict) that Jesus is the Christ" (I John 2:22). They crucify Him again (Revelation 11:8, Hebrews 6:6). Such a man is the antichrist—*"he denies the Father and the Son"* (I John 2:22). Any former follower of Christ who embraces another religion and deny Christ Jesus, they are antichrists. Do not trust them they are liars (John 2:24-25). They are false prophets.

The false prophet of Revelation 13:11 is the spirit behind every false religion, and he likes to seduce followers of Christ. The false prophets' main target is to try to deceive the *"elect"* of God (Matthews 24:24). Remember, *"No one who denies the Son has the Father"* (I John 2:23).

Anyone who claims they are serving the same God as Christians, but deny Jesus Christ as being the Son of God is an antichrist. The scripture quoted above said that if Jesus is being denied as **The Christ,** then they are not serving the same ***"Father."*** Another aspect of the antichrist is the fact that they deny Jesus *"as coming in the flesh."*

II John 1:7, NIV:
*Many deceivers, who do not acknowledge Jesus Christ **as coming** in the flesh, have gone out into the world. Any such person is the deceiver and the antichrist.*

II John 1:7, KJV:
*For many deceivers are entered into the world, who confess not that Jesus Christ **is** come in the flesh. This is a deceiver and an antichrist.*

The antichrists are those who do not acknowledge that, *"Jesus Christ **is** come in the flesh"* (KJV). The little word **"is"** is an emphasis of this scripture. There are many people who refuse to believe that Jesus **is** the Son of God who **came in the flesh.** *"And without controversy great is the mystery of godliness: **God was manifest in the flesh,** justified in the Spirit, seen of*

16

angels, preached unto the Gentiles, believed on in the world, received up into glory" (I Timothy 3:16, KJV).

Jesus, the Christ did come in the flesh, He died on the cross, and He is resurrected at the right hand of God. There is more though, he **is** still coming in the flesh. Jesus in his omnipresence is also living in the body (flesh) of his Church.

The antichrists are those who refuse to believe that Jesus is living in us—the Church. Jesus Christ **is** come in the flesh. That is, he is come in flesh of the Church. The Holy Writ says, *"To them [Saints] God has chosen to make known among the Gentiles the glorious riches of this mystery, which is Christ in you, the hope of glory"* (Colossians 1:27). The *"Spirit of Jesus"* is in us **now** (I Corinthians 3:16, NIV, NASB with Acts 16:7, NIV, NASB).

"And if anyone does not have the Spirit of Christ, he does not belong to Christ"* (Romans 8:9).** All who deny that Jesus is living in the flesh of His Church now is antichrist. They do ***"not belong to Christ." Therefore, watch those pseudo saints and so called prophets who have a doctrine that deny that Jesus is come in the flesh. He came literally ~2000 years ago and spiritually in us presently. An application of this denial of Jesus coming in the flesh is the one who says, "The Holy Spirit manifesting in our body by the evidence of speaking in tongues is evil, or demonic." I guess they have not read Mark 3:28-30.

Mark 3:28-30 teach that anyone who says that the work being done by the Holy Sprit is unclean or demonic is saying an unpardonable sin *(The best Greek text for* Mark 3:29 *reads:* ***"eternal sin"*** *as can be seen in the New International Version and the New American Standard—Updated Edition)* —look it up. There are many false brethren and false prophets among the saints. They like Jannes and Jambres—the two sorcerers who opposed Moses—are resisting the truth of the power of God. But they will go no further. They only have limited power.

CHAPTER 2
THE DRAGON'S TAIL

Revelation 12:3-4, NIV:
*³ Then another sign appeared in heaven: an enormous red dragon with seven heads and ten horns and seven crowns on his heads. ⁴ **His tail swept a third of the stars out of the sky and flung them to the earth.** The dragon stood in front of the woman who was about to give birth, so that he might devour her child the moment it was born.*

The dragon in the book of Revelation used his tail to fling a third part of the stars of heaven to the earth. This dragon is a corporate entity **(See Volume 1—The False Prophet, Alias, Another Beast).** His seven heads are seven ruling angels—who dominate some so called *"elders"* and *"prominent men."* The dragon's ***"tail"*** is a metaphor for the *"many false prophets."* This is seen in **God's** statement through Isaiah.

Isaiah 9:15, NIV:
*The elders and prominent men are the head, the **prophets who teach lies are the tail.***

This is a revealing statement. *"Prophets who teach **lies** are the **tail.**"* Jesus also says that false believers and false leaders have a liar for a father. Jesus said, *"You belong to your father, the devil... for he is **a liar** and **the father of lies"* (John 8:44).** The Devil is a liar and the father of lies. Therefore, ministers that *"teach lies"* are fathered by Satan. Do you see the connection? Metaphorically, the teachers who teach lies are the *"tail."* What tail? The **tail of the dragon!** Do you see this? If not, as you read this chapter, it will become clearer. There was great man who had to deal with a serpent's tail, his name is Moses.

Moses had to take up a *"snake"* by the *"tail."* In the New Testament, the word dragon used in the book of Revelation means *"a large **serpent"*** (See Vines). As we will see in a moment, what Moses did with the serpent's tail, points to the fact that he would take the dragons of Egypt by their tails. It is the same way in this generation. The apostles and prophets of God must take the dragon by the tail to stop its lies. We must stop it from throwing down the **stars—saints—**to the ground with his lies (See referenced verses where stars are used symbolically to represent saints: Genesis 37:9-10; Daniel 12:3; Matthew 2:1-2; Philippians 2:14-15).

MOSES AND THE SERPENT'S TAIL

Exodus 4:2-5, NIV:
*² Then the LORD said to him, "What is that in your hand?" "A staff," he replied. ³ The LORD said, "Throw it on the ground." Moses threw it on the ground and it became a snake and he ran from it. ⁴ Then the LORD said to him, **"Reach out your hand and take it by the tail."** So Moses reached out and took hold of the snake*

and it turned back into a staff in his hand. [5] *"This," said the LORD, "is so that they may believe that the LORD, the God of their fathers—the God of Abraham, the God of Isaac and the God of Jacob—has appeared to you."*

The man, Moses was empowered by our Lord to go into Egypt and deliver the people of God. God knew he was destined to encounter some of the **false powers** of Egypt. Therefore God prepared him. Moses had some concerns about the people's beliefs in the fact that God had indeed sent him. In the process of God strengthening Moses, God would empower him to take the *"snake"* by the *"tail."* God had turned Moses' staff into a *"snake."* He then commanded Moses to take up the snake by the *"tail." **Principle:** In these days those who can take the dragon by his tail will validate their ministry that the Head of the Church has sent them* (Exodus 4:5).

As we learned earlier in this chapter, the tail of the snake is emblematic of the false prophets. In Moses' case, the tail of the serpent was symbolic of the sorcerers (false prophets) of Egypt—a type of the world. The Hebrew for **"snake"** means, a snake from its hiss; to whisper a (magic) spell; to prognosticate; divine, enchanter, (use) enchantment, etc. (Strong's Concordance # 5175 & 5172).

Thus the snake points to the witches of Egypt who Moses would defeat. It is with Moses' encounter with the sorcerers/false prophets of Egypt I will use to show the limited power of the dragon's tail. Before I discuss this *"limited power,"* I will show how in this age that there is a **present** application of Moses' encounter with the *"tail"* of the serpent.

Peter talked about being *"established in the present truth"* (II Peter 1:12, KJV). All the **truths** of the Bible can be applied to our **present** season. We are **presently** in the *"terrible times in the last days."* However, like Moses, we will know the ways of God which will enable us to function in the works of God.

II Timothy 3:1-9, NIV:

[1]*But mark this: **There will be terrible times in the last days**.* [2] *People will be lovers of themselves, lovers of money, boastful, proud, abusive, disobedient to their parents, ungrateful, unholy,* [3] *without love, unforgiving, slanderous, without self-control, brutal, not lovers of the good,* [4] *treacherous, rash, conceited, lovers of pleasure rather than lovers of God—* [5] *having a form of godliness but denying its power. Have nothing to do with them.* [6] *They are the kind who worm their way into homes and gain control over weak-willed women, who are loaded down with sins and are swayed by all kinds of evil desires,* [7] *always learning but never able to acknowledge the truth.* [8] *Just as **Jannes and Jambres** opposed Moses, so also these **men oppose the truth**—men of depraved minds, who, as far as the faith is concerned, are rejected.* [9] *But they will not get very far because, as in the case of those men, their folly will be clear to everyone.*

Paul said, *"**Mark this: There will be** terrible times in the last days."* There is a mark that distinguishes the

22

terrible times in the last days. There is a *"mark"* that will be **"in"** the *"last days."* Another way of saying it is: The last days will be marked or recognized by certain prevailing attitudes.

Listen: *"People will be lovers of themselves."* Does this describe the world and some in the Church today? People will be *"lovers of money, boastful, proud, abusive,"* etc. Sounds like this age doesn't it? There is also another mark of the last days, children being *"disobedient to their parents."* Does this describe the world today? The list goes on: *"lovers of pleasure rather than lovers of God"* (Contrast Hebrews 11:24-25). You and I both know that the list given by the apostle describes this age exactly.

That means that we are *"in the last days."* Paul called these days *"terrible times."* He did not stop there. He said, ***"Have nothing to do with them."*** Why was the beloved apostle so harsh? It appears that he is describing most people in the world. Therefore, who can be saved—Matthew 19:25-26—if we are to *"have nothing to do with them?"*

The understanding is: he compared these people to Jannes and Jambres who were Egypt's sorcerers that withstood Moses. The Scripture says, ***"Just as Jannes and Jambres opposed Moses ..."*** (II Timothy 3:8). *The* **attitudes that Paul lists springs out of sorcery, witchcraft, warlocks, wizardry, psychic, necromancy, diviners, them that has familiar spirits, etc.** According to the book of Deuteronomy, we are commanded not to associate with people who are sorcerers or use sorcery (Deuteronomy 18:9-14). This is why the Spirit of Jesus through Paul was so assertive—*"have nothing to do with them."* There is a dark power behind the attitudes Paul listed above. In other words, the same attitude that the sorcerers of that age displayed against Moses is the same attitude this age has against God and His saints; and it is manifested through **all** who has contact with the lawless powers similar to that of the two sorcerers of Egypt.

This truth also shows the lifestyle people live in secret. This kind of attitude stems out of contacts with sorcerers. In other words, the reason why these attitudes are treated so harshly by Paul is because they stem from the secret art of sorcery and contact with any form of the secret sects of the this present darkness. Let us now see how sorcery—the tail (Jannes and Jambres) of Pharaoh—were defeated by Moses. I will begin by defining the meaning of the *"two horns"* that was discussed in Chapter 1.

*"Then I saw another beast, coming out of the earth. He had **two horns** like a lamb, but he spoke like a dragon"* (Revelation 13:11, NIV). Remember the true Lamb of God has seven horns (Revelation 5). Seven in the Hebrew means, "complete" (See Strong's Concordance). Therefore, Jesus has complete power and authority (Matthew 28:18). It follows that the beast of Revelation 13: 11 has **limited**—power. He only has **two** horns.

Therefore one of the applications of the two horns is: they are figurative of limited power—the limited power of the Devil. Now, allow me to qualify the statement above. The power of the devil is limited when it comes to dealing with the people of God (John 14:30;

24

Colossians 1:13; Job 1:12; Job 2:6). However for those who deny the truth, God will allow *"the working of Satan with **all power** and signs and lying wonders"* to deceive all who reject the **Truth—personified in Jesus** (See II Thessalonians 2:1-12). The NIV says Satan will display *"**all** kinds of counterfeit miracles, signs and wonders."* However, when it comes to the saints, the powers of darkness are **limited.** The false prophets only have two horns, not seven. Let us see.

LIMITED POWERS OF EGYPT

Exodus 7:8-9, NIV:
*[8] The LORD said to Moses and Aaron, [9] "When Pharaoh says to you, 'Perform a miracle, 'then say to Aaron, 'Take your staff and throw it down before Pharaoh,' and it will become a **snake.***

The Lord asked the man Moses to do the same thing with this staff that he had done with God on the mountain—*"throw it down before Pharaoh, and it will become a **snake.**"* This time (Exodus 7:9) the Hebrew word for *"snake" (tanniy,* or *tanniym—Strong's Old Testament: 8577)* is not the same word for *"snake" (nachash—Strong's Old Testament: 5175)* in Exodus 4:3. The word snake in Exodus 7:9 is also translated as ***"dragon"*** in the King James Version.

Ezekiel 29:3, KJV:
*Speak, and say, Thus saith the Lord GOD; Behold, I am against thee, **Pharaoh** king of Egypt, the **great dragon***

(Hebrew, tanniyn, or tanniym) that lieth in the midst of his rivers, which hath said, My river is mine own, and I have made it for myself.

Isaiah 27:1, KJV:
In that day the LORD with his sore and great and strong sword shall punish leviathan the piercing serpent, even leviathan that crooked serpent; and he shall slay the dragon (Hebrew, tanniyn, or tanniym) that is in the sea.

In other words, the first time Moses threw his staff down it became **a serpent.** The second time the staff became **a dragon.** The first time Moses picked up the serpent by the **tail.** This time he will again pick up the dragons of Egypt by the tail, except, in a different way. Moses will use the unmatched power of God to take the two representatives of Egypt by their *"tails."* In modern vernacular, Moses is going to *"kick some tail."* Yes! Yes! Application: The Church will also kick the dragon's tail. Let us see how this will be accomplished. After Moses' staff had turned into the dragon (Exodus 7:10), Pharaoh's sorcerers did the same.

Exodus 7:11-12, NIV:
[11] *Pharaoh then summoned wise men and sorcerers, and the Egyptian magicians also **did the same things by their secret arts:** [12] Each one threw down his staff and it became a snake (lit; dragon). **But Aaron's staff swallowed up their staffs.***

The sorcerers and magicians *"also did the same thing."* Except, they use the **secret** arts of the Devil. They used enchantment (King James Version). *"The secret power of lawlessness is already at work"* (II Thessalonians 2:7). ***Principle:*** *In this age, there are some acts of God that false prophets will copy by the "secret power" or "secret arts" of the devil* (Revelation 13:12-13; Revelation 16:14; Deuteronomy 13:1-2; Revelation 13:15 with Genesis 2:7).

Now you can understand why John was so firm: *"Dear friends, **do not believe every** spirit, but test the spirits to see whether they are from God, because many false prophets have gone out into the world"* (I John 4:1). Paul was even stronger than John. He said, ***"Have nothing to do with them" (II Timothy 3:5).***

Now the fact that the magicians copied Moses was not the only thing that was stated. Moses and Aaron's staff eventually *"swallowed up"* the sorcerers' staffs. Remember that I said above that Moses' staff turned into a "dragon." I also said that this fact is significant to know. The point is this. Moses' staff that turned into a dragon swallowed up the two dragons of Egypt.

The strength of God's power is demonstrated in the fact that Moses' staff swallowed up two crocodiles, not mere snakes. The sorcerers and magicians copied Moses. But their powers were limited. They could only copy. But God's **all power** swallowed up their **limited power.** Listen to the scripture: *"But Aaron's staff swallowed up their staffs."*

The snake in scripture is also symbolic of **shrewdness.** Jesus said, *"Be as **shrewd** as **snakes** and as innocent as doves"* (Matthews 10:16). The snakes of Egypt are also a metaphor of the *"shrewdness"* of the world. However, the wisdom of God will take the shrewdness of this world by the tail and swallow it up. The false prophets' wisdom of this world is limited. God took the snakes (crocodiles or dragons) of Egypt by their tails.

*"Oh, **the depth** of the riches of **the wisdom** and knowledge of God! How unsearchable his judgments, and his paths **beyond** tracing out! **"Who has known the mind of the Lord? Or who has been his counselor"*** (Romans 11:33-34)? Jannes and Jambres must have been stunned. This was only the beginning of their demise. This was the first of three demonstrations by God that the power of the dragon's tail is limited, and is swallowed up by Jesus.

COPYING IS LIMITED

II Corinthians 11:13-15, NIV:
[13] *For such men are false apostles, deceitful workmen, masquerading as apostles of Christ.* [14] *And no wonder, for **Satan himself masquerades as an angel of light.*** [15] *It is not surprising, then, if **his** servants **masquerade** as servants of righteousness. Their end will be what their actions deserve.*

Copying is one of Satan's deceptive ways. He has appeared unto many false prophets as *"an **angel** of* *light."* The Bible said not to listen to any *"man"* or *"angel"* who brings another gospel (Galatians 1:8-9). Fallen angels, especially Satan, bring false light or pseudo religion. ***"It is not surprising, then,*** *if his servants masquerade as servants of righteousness."* Jannes and Jambres did the same thing. They also **masquerade** God's power. That is, they masquerade their power as the power of God. However, God only allowed it for **three times—Exodus 7:12—snake; 7:21-22—blood and 8:6-7—frogs)**—and that was it. God allowed the satanic power of the sorcerers to work for a season to deceive Pharaoh with the energy of error that his heart should be hardened.

The Holy Writ says, *"And for this cause God shall send them **strong delusion (lit; energy of error),** that they should believe a lie"* (II Thessalonians 2:11, KJV). *Why did God allow this?* *"That they all might be damned who **believed not the truth,** but had pleasure in unrighteousness"* (II Thessalonians 2:12, KJV). The *"truth"* that Pharaoh did not believe was that our God is the only God (Exodus 5:2). Thus God allowed this lying energy to work **three** times.

In Revelation 16: 13-14, it was *"three"* unclean spirits that were allowed to perform false miracles. This points to the fact that in the same way God allowed the false sorcerers and magicians of Egypt to be limited to three copies, the evil spirits that perform miracles are also limited to three—the dragon, the beast and the false prophets (Revelation 16:13-14).

Principle: *In this age it appears that the world's false prophets—psychics, the palm readers,*

29

necromancers, warlocks, sorcerers, Satan worshippers, wizards (male witches), witches, New Age Movement, false teachers in the Church, etc, can copy God's power and God's prophetic in a limited way. However, God will stymie the false ones. The question must be asked then, why does God allow this falsehood to continue?

HARD HEARTS

Exodus 7:22, NIV:
*But the Egyptian magicians did the same things by their secret arts, and **Pharaoh's heart became hard;** he would not listen to Moses and Aaron, just as the LORD had said.*

II Thessalonians 2:11-12, NIV:
*[11] For this reason God sends them a **powerful delusion** so that they will believe **the lie** [12] and so that all will be condemned who have not believed the **truth** but have delighted in wickedness.*

In II Thessalonians 2:9-10, God will allow false miracles to occur. **Why? It will be for those who have not believed the truth—a person named Jesus.** Therefore, God will send *"them a **powerful delusion** (lit.; energy of error) to believe **the lie.**"* Allow me to make the above statements practical. God is allowing the false prophets of the world to perform their false miracles. False signs are energizing the words of the false prophets. This will harden the hearts of those who refuse to believe the truth of Jesus. The Devil through is fake agencies will cause people who listen to him to become hard against God.

They are saying, "The things I am hearing in the world from the psychics and witches are coming to past. Therefore, why should I follow Jesus? I can have the pleasures of the world and prophetic insight." Thus, their hearts are hardened, and the scripture—II Thessalonians 2:11-12—is fulfilled. God is allowing them to believe the *"energy"* of *"the lie"* that they may be *"condemned,"* according to II Thessalonians 2:11-12. I plead with you. If you are involved with the psychics, witches, warlock, palm-readers, etc, of this dark-age stop! Turn to God, and do not harden your heart. Receive Jesus—Now! It is possible to get victory over the beast (Revelation 15:2).

God hardened Pharaoh's heart for the same reason. It was after the sorcerer and magicians performed their false miracle that the Holy Writ said that Pharaoh became harder in his heart. Listen to the scripture again: *"But the Egyptian magicians did the same things by their secret arts,* **and** *Pharaoh's heart became hard; he would not listen to Moses and Aaron, just as the LORD had said"* (Exodus 7:22).

Notice the conjunction *"and."* It connects the first and second statements in the scripture. Do you see that? God hardened Pharaoh's heart when he believed the secret arts (power) of the dragon instead of God's power. The same thing will happen to you if you refuse God's power (I Corinthians 1:18 and 1:24, etc) and choose Satan's. Remember, the power of sorcery is limited. There are things that our Lord Jesus Christ has reserved that nothing false can copy.

"THEY COULD NOT"

Exodus 8:16-18, NIV:
*[16] Then the LORD said to Moses, "Tell Aaron, `Stretch out your staff and strike the dust of the ground,' and throughout the land of Egypt the dust will become gnats." [17] They did this, and when Aaron stretched out his hand with the staff and struck the dust of the ground, gnats came upon men and animals. All the dust throughout the land of Egypt became gnats. [18] But when the magicians tried to produce gnats by their secret arts, **they could not.** And the gnats were on men and animals.*

God showed the magicians who is all-powerful. ***God is all-powerful!*** They tried to copy God for the fourth time, and *"they could not."* This *"present evil age"* (Galatians 1:4) will try to copy God. However in the words' of Paul, *"they will not get very far"* (II Timothy 3:9). The powers of the false prophets are limited. They may reproduce for a while. But one day, all the false prophets of the world will acknowledge that God's finger is all-powerful.

The magicians said to Pharaoh, *"This is the finger of God"* (Exodus 8:19). Yes! Yes! Yes! Jesus said he cast out demons by the *"finger of God"* (Luke 11:20). Matthew's record calls the *"finger of God" "the Spirit of God"* (Matthews 12:28). In Revelation 16: 13-14, the limited power of three evil (lit.; unclean) spirits also

32

performed false miracles. But one day, the world will acknowledge that The **Holy** *(The Greek for "Holy" is:* **Hagios** *which also means,* **Clean or Pure)** **Spirit** is all-powerful (Revelation 11:11-13; Philippians 2:10-11). *"The Finger of God,"* which is the Holy or Pure Spirit of God, can do things that **unclean** spirits cannot do. *"The Finger of God,"* through his prophets, will take the dragon by his tail. Make sure that it is the "Clean" Spirit of God who is doing the miracles not "unclean" spirits (Compare Revelation 16:14). I reiterate: The fact that the magicians *"could not"* copy the act of producing lice showed that God through Moses had taken the two dragons of Egypt by the tail. The Lord God stymied the two *"tails"* of Egypt. Satan's power is limited. Do not allow the fake powers of false prophets to seduce you into following the darkness that exists in this age!

Understand that psychics, palm readers, necromancers, warlocks, sorcerers, Satan worshippers, wizards—male witches, witches, new age movement, false teachers in the Church, etc, are limited in what they can do or say to a true disciple. They have an end. *"Their **end** will be what their actions deserve"* (II Corinthians 11:15b). The *"tail"* of the dragon will be exposed for what it is—the many false prophets (II Timothy 3:9).

Now before I conclude, I will give a brief review of the **other two** acts of Moses that the false prophets of Egypt copied and show how the false ones of this dark-age cause the same verdicts to trap this generation. Above I indicated that God only allowed the sorcerers to copy Moses for three **times—Exodus 7:12—snake;**

7:21-22—blood and 8:6-7—frogs)—and that was it. I canvassed the *"snake"* briefly. I will now canvass the *"blood"* and the *"frog."*

The question is: "What is the principle behind the blood being reproduced by the false prophets of Egypt?" I will explain it this way. Moses produced blood that caused death and a foul smell in Egypt (Exodus 7:21). God is doing the same thing in this age. Blood shed is increasing in the land until it becomes foul. Then God will judge the bloodshed (Isaiah 26:20-21). Blood has to do with covenant. Abuse of blood brought *"punishment."* For Example, those who abuse the blood of Jesus will get punished.

Hebrews 10:29, NIV:
*How much more severely do you think a man deserves to be **punished** who has trampled the Son of God under foot, who has treated as an unholy thing the **blood of the covenant** that sanctified him, and who has insulted the Spirit of grace?*

If the Church abuses the blood of Jesus there is punishment associated with that abuse. God does not like the abuse of blood in any form. God even demands the *"accounting from every animal"* that shed blood (Genesis 9:4-6). This is the truth. God judged Egypt with blood because they were shedding blood. There are many *"so-called"* religions and secret societies that require the shedding of blood for initiation into their beliefs.

This bloodshed ranges from "branding" to literal murdering of humanity. The druids sacrificed children annually worshiping Satan, Baal, or Molech (Ezekiel 16:21, Leviticus 18:21, Isaiah 57:3-5, etc). Remember the four hundred and fifty "prophets of Baal"—I King 18:25—when they encountered Elijah (I Kings 18:19-40). Listen to what they did when their limited power was being exposed by Elijah: *"So they shouted louder and **slashed themselves** with swords and spears, as was their custom, until **their blood** flowed"* (II Kings 18:28).

The many forms of witchcraft and divination use blood as an initiation—animals to humans. Diviners use the *"liver"* for divination (Ezekiel 21:21). This means an animal had to shed blood for them to get the liver. What is my point? God judged Egypt with blood because they were shedding blood in the land with all their abominable practices. In Genesis 9:5 God says that he requires an *"accounting"* for lifeblood. It is so serious to God that if an animal kills a man that animal must give an account to God. *"And for **your** lifeblood I will surely demand an accounting. I will demand an accounting from **every animal**. And from **each** man, **too**, I will demand an accounting for the life of his fellow man"* (Genesis 9:5). People's bloodshed is serious to God. Therefore, all who abuse blood is forming a covenant with the devil; and they must give an account. The false prophets and all who shed blood in the world will be judged by blood similarly to Egypt, if they do not turn from their evil practices and become a disciple of Jesus. Listen to the Revelation of Jesus Christ.

Revelation 8:7, NIV:
*The first angel sounded his trumpet, and there came **hail and fire mixed with blood,** and it was hurled down upon the earth. A third of the earth was burned up, a third of the trees were burned up, and all the green grass was burned up.*

Revelation 8:8-9, NIV:
*[8] The second angel sounded his trumpet, and something like a huge mountain, all ablaze, was thrown into the sea. A third of the **sea turned into blood,** [9] a third of the living creatures in the sea died, and a third of the ships were destroyed.*

Revelation 16:3-7, NIV:
*[3] The second angel poured out his bowl on the sea, and it turned into **blood** like that of a dead man, and every living thing in the sea died. [4] The third angel poured out his bowl on the rivers and springs of water, and they became **blood.** [5] Then I heard the angel in charge of the waters say: "You are just in these judgments, you who are and who were, the Holy One, because you have so judged; [6] **for they have shed the blood** of your saints and prophets, and you have given them **blood** to drink as they deserve." [7] **And I heard the altar respond: "Yes, Lord God Almighty, true and just are your judgments."***

God judged Egypt with blood because of the innocent blood they shed when they killed the *"boy"* children of the Jews (Exodus 1:15-22). The Egyptian were shedding the blood of God's Church of that day

(Israel in the days of Moses were also called "Church" Acts 7:38). They were trying to get to the seed—Moses. The world shall be judged in the same manner for doing the same thing. The blood of the prophets and saints shall be accounted for by the world. Even, the prophets killed in/by abortionist **before** they were born. Prophets do not become prophets over night. God placed them in their mother's womb as prophets (Jeremiah 1:5).

A sign that the seed of God is being birth in this season is the escalation of abortion in the earth. The dragon is trying to kill the seed of God personally and through humans (Revelation 12; Matthew 2:1-18; Exodus 1:15-22). Remember in the book of Revelation they were given blood to drink because they shed blood. Listen to the scripture. *"For they have shed the blood of your saints and prophets, and you have given them blood to drink as they deserve" (Revelation 16:6).*

I will now conclude with the frogs. There are spirits that **look like** frogs. The strange thing about this truth is that the dragon, the beast and the false prophet have their own frog spirits. Yet, at least two of them do not **look** like a frog.

Revelation 16:12-14, NIV:
[12] The sixth angel poured out his bowl on the great river Euphrates, and its water was dried up to prepare the way for the kings from the East. [13] Then I saw three evil spirits that looked like frogs; they came out of the mouth of the dragon, out of the mouth of the beast and out of the mouth of the false prophet.

As seen in the verses above, the *"frogs"* of Egypt can point to *"the evil (lit.; unclean) spirits that looked like frogs."* A note in passing: I could expound on the gods of Egypt that had animal heads with human bodies. The Egyptians had a god with a frog's head. I suggest you study them in contrast of the cherubs of God (Ezekiel 1). One symbolism of the frogs was the fact that Egypt had *"unclean sprits"* in their land. In light of Revelation 16:13a, the frogs that Moses produced points to *"evil or unclean spirits"* that judged Egypt. The purpose of the frogs was to judge Egypt for all their uncleanness.

Principle: *The very unclean thing a person uses, God will cause it to multiply in judgment against the user.* This is what God did to Egypt. Egypt worshipped frogs, therefore, God judged them by frogs. In the book of Revelation 16:13, the dragon multiplied by reproducing a frog spirit. The beast did the same thing and so did the false prophets. All those who indulge with false prophets—psychics, the palm readers, necromancers, warlocks, sorcerers, Satan worshippers, wizards (male witches), witches, new age movement, false teachers, etc, in the Church will be judged by the same secret arts they use.

God will cause the life of the indulgers to be tormented miserable by the **stench** of uncleanness for using unclean spirits (Exodus 8:13). The Lord, through his Church judging the false prophets, shall take the dragon by his tail and expose the prophets who teach lies. Why? He wants to deliver the oppressed.

It is never too late to stop unclean indulgencies with false prophets. You can be saved. The blood of Jesus is stronger than any blood that may have you bound by a false covenant. Do not believe the lie that you were born or destined to be a witch, warlock, necromancer, etc (Acts 19:18-19, NIV). The road to freedom may not be easy for **you**— and I emphasize **"you."** However, our God is all-powerful. All things are possible with Him, including your deliverance from every evil covenant.

Matthew 19:26, NIV:
Jesus looked at them and said, "With man this is impossible, but with God all things are possible."

He will protect you. Once you get saved in truth, our God will hide you in Christ Jesus. Colossians 3:1-4 says that after we believe in the Lord Jesus and seek those things that are above in heaven, we will be *"hidden with Christ in God."* Psalms 91: 4 say, *"He will cover you with his feathers, and under his wings you will find refuge; his faithfulness will be your shield and rampart."*

Now there are two things I must develop in the subsequent chapters. The lie must be explained and the rest of the process by which God will expose the false prophets in this present evil age.

CHAPTER 3
THE LIE

Revelation 13:14-15, NIV:
*[14] Because of the signs he was given power to do on behalf of the first beast, he deceived the inhabitants of the earth. He ordered them to set up **an image** in honor of the beast who was wounded by the sword and yet lived. [15] He was given power to give breath to the image of the first beast, so that it could speak and cause all who refused to **worship the image** to be killed.*

Revelation 13:4, NIV:
*Men **worshiped the dragon** because he had given authority to the beast, and they also **worshiped the beast** and asked, "Who is like the beast? Who can make war against him?"*

Romans 1:25, NIV:
*They exchanged the truth of God for **a lie (lit.; the lie)**, and worshiped and served **created things** rather than the **Creator**-who is forever praised. Amen.*

What is *"the lie,"* and what does it have to do with "worship." In the mind of most people when the word "lie" is mentioned, they probably think of "a fib." This is partially true. However, *"the lie"* is a little deeper than that. It has to do with men (who are *"created things"*) worshiping the beast and dragon

40

(*"created things"*) (Romans 1:25; Revelation 13:4). The emphasis being placed on *"created things."* Before I explain the lie in detail with reference to worship of the created things rather than the Creator, I will show how *"the lie"* is linked to the false prophets, for continuity.

The liar is *"the man who **denies** that Jesus is the Christ. Such a man is the **antichrist**—he denies the father and the* son" *(I John 2:22).* The antichrist is the liar. I John 4:1-3 teach that the *"many false prophets"* are *"the spirit of antichrist."* One can logically conclude that the false prophets are one of the faces of the antichrists. The antichrists are *"the liars."* I John 2:22 ask, *"Who is **the** liar?"* The same verse then gave the answer: *"It is the man who denies (or contradicts) that Jesus is the Christ."*

Therefore, the Devil, who is the father of lies, must have denied the **God/Man** Jesus in the beginning (Good study). It is from this point of view, I will expound to you the lie. A purpose of my expounding this lie is to keep you from falsehood. I have taught this to a degree in Volume I—*The False Prophet, Alias, Another Beast.* Therefore on the most part, I will teach in this chapter that which was not included in the first volume.

SPEAKING FROM HIS OWN

John 8:44, NIV:
You belong to your father, the devil, and you want to carry out your father's desire. He was a murderer from the beginning, not holding to the truth, for there is no

truth in him. When he lies, he speaks his native language, for he is a liar and the father of lies.

John 8:44, KJV:
*Ye are of your father the devil, and the lusts of your father ye will do. He was a murderer from the beginning, and abode not in the truth, because there is no truth in him. When he speaketh a lie, **he speaketh of his own:** for he is a liar, and the father of it.*

The lie is a very serious topic. It is link to what I call "the deepest statement Jesus said." Before we look at that statement let us look at a portion of John 8:44 in the King James Version: *"When he [the Devil] speaketh a lie (Greek; the lie), he speaketh of (Greek; ek, out of) his own."* Therefore speaking *"the lie"* has to do with speaking *"out of"* ones *"own"* self. Our Lord Jesus is opposite the statement above. Listen to what I believe is one of the deepest statements Jesus said.

John 5:30, KJV:
I can of mine own self do nothing: *as I hear, I judge: and my judgment is just; because **I seek not mine own will,** but the will of the Father which hath sent me.*

You may say "Brother Peart why is this statement so 'deep'?" Jesus said, *"I can **of** mine **own** self do nothing."* The word *"of"* means: *"from"* in the Greek. The verse should read, *"I can **'from'** mine own self do nothing."* This means that Jesus did nothing that **originated** from himself. Every single thing that he did, it was because, the Father told Him to do it, or He saw His father do it (John 5:19). In other words the statement is talking about absolute reliance on God's approval to do a task before the task is embarked upon. Jesus did absolutely **nothing** on His own.

Jesus' statement is deep because we would not sin if we stop living *"from"* our own self. It is deep because; it means absolute death to self. It is deep because we are not living this truth absolutely. If we were not seeking our *"own will"* all of the Father's will would be done in earth as it is being done in the heavens. Anything that has its origin *"from"* fallen mankind and fallen angels is *"the lie."*

Remember, the lie of the Devil is that he speaks *"out of"* his *"own"* selves. The Church, through grace, must live opposite the lie of the Devil. We like Jesus must do nothing from our self. We must seek His will. False prophets are the opposite and always speak from themselves.

Ezekiel 13:1-3, NIV:
*[1] The word of the LORD came to me: [2] "Son of man, prophecy against the prophets of Israel who are now prophesying. Say to those who prophesy out of their **own** imagination: 'Hear the word of the LORD! [3] This is what the Sovereign LORD says: Woe to the foolish prophets who follow their **own** spirit and have seen nothing!*

This is the difference between the Devil's prophets and God's holy prophets. The Devil's prophets do what the Devil does. They speak out of their *"own"* imagination. They follow their *"own"* spirits, which are unclean. Thus, they are liars. The Lord controls the spirits of the true prophets. He is the God of the spirits of the true prophets.

"The angel said to me, 'These words are trustworthy and true. **The Lord, the God of the spirits of the prophets,** *sent his angel to show his servants the things that must soon take place'"* (Revelation 22:6, NIV). There is something special to God about the spirit of the true prophets of God. They have submitted their spirits to the living God (Romans 1:9, II Timothy 4:22, Philemon 25). They do not *"speak from their own self."* They are only *"carried along"* or *"moved"* by the Holy Spirit (II Peter 1:21). Prophets whose spirits are controlled by the Lord do not have their own interpretation.

IDIOTS

II Peter 1:20-21, NIV
[20] Above all, you must understand that no prophecy of Scripture came about by the prophet's **own interpretation.** *[21] For prophecy never had its origin in the will of man, but men spoke from God as they were carried along by the Holy Spirit.*

The word *"own"* is the Greek "idias." The word "idiot" is from this Greek word and is used several place in the New Testament (Greek for: ignorant—Acts 4:13, KJV; II Peter 3:5; 3:8, KJV; Greek for rude—II Corinthians 11:6, KJV). In ancient Greek culture, it was customary to go to the square and confer with at least two or three persons on topics. An **idiot** was an individual who would not confer with the group. He would go off to himself and have his own private interpretation—ideas. Thus, false prophets are idiots with there own ideas.

They only listen to the thoughts of their **own** hearts. There is no communion between their spirits and the God of the **spirits** of all mankind (Numbers 16:22, Jeremiah 23:21-22). The Holy Spirit says, *"How long will this continue in the hearts of these **lying prophets,** who prophesy the delusions of their **own** minds"* (Jeremiah 23:26)? False prophets, like Satan, speak from their own minds.

They do not gather with the Godhead—Father, Son and Holy Spirit—to receive words from God. Instead, they seek counsel from their own fallen heart. They refuse the *"counsel"* of the Lord (Jeremiah 23:22). According to Peter, they are idiots. "Okay Brother Peart I hear you, but how do I know when prophets are idiots—speaking from their own selves?"

John 7:17-18, NIV:
*If anyone **chooses to do God's will,** he will find out whether my teaching comes from (**Gk.; "ek"—out of)** God or whether I speak on (**Gk.; "Apo"—from)** my own.* [18] *He who speaks **on (Gk.; from)** his **own** does so to gain honor for himself, but he who works for the honor of the one who sent him is a man of truth; there is nothing false about him.*

Jesus gave the answer as to how to know those who are speaking, or teaching from their own heart and mind. Remember, idiots are like the Devil who was the first to speak from his own private (ideological) interpretation concerning himself (see my booklet, *When God Made Satan*). Concerning the true believer, Jesus said, *"There is nothing false about him"*—the one who works for God's honor (John 7:18). If there is *"nothing false"* about the man who does God's will, there must be *"something false"* about those who speak and do things from themselves.

The answer the Lord gave may be subjective to you if you are not spiritual. That is, the way a person knows God's teaching is by choosing God's will. It is not ascertained by physical appearance. Jesus said, *"If anyone chooses to do God's will...."*—*the Greek structure of this phrase reads, "If anyone chooses His choice he will know."*

The key to **knowing** if a preacher, false prophets, etc are speaking from themselves is to **choose God's choice for your life.** This means: that which God has chosen for your life accept it and you will be able to discern doctrine. Everyone—deep, deep, deep in their hearts know what is God's choice for their lives. God's choices include general directives or time specific directives. Do you understand?

As we choose God's choices, the Church will be able to distinguish between the ones who are prophesying from their own heart rather than the heart of God. This kind of discernment is internal. You cannot concentrate on how a person looks and dress. They may

46

have the finest clothes, finest cars, and houses. Or, they may be a person who does not dress so well, poor, etc. Outward appearance cannot be the ultimate measure (I Samuel 16:7). All the sincere ones must choose Jesus' choice to be able to understand doctrine whether the doctrine is of God. We—the Church—must reevaluate ourselves.

We must see if all the things we say God said is true or not. A good friend of mine—Steve Daniel—said that he decided to write down every thing that would "appear" to be God speaking to him for a certain period. He did this for approximately eight months. After the eight months, he concluded that if God had told him to do all the things he wrote down, God would have been confused and crazy. His point was to show that we should not follow everything that comes into our *"own"* heart. The Church must not be so quick to say, "God said" and God did not say. False prophets, according to Ezekiel and Jeremiah, speak from their own hearts and not from the heart of God (Jeremiah 28:2). They claim to hear from God (Jeremiah 28:2), however, these false prophets hear lies (Jeremiah 28:15-17; 27:9-10; 23:9-18).

Now, as stated in the beginning of this chapter, I will show through the Word how the lie is linked to creature worship. In John 8:44 (KJV) Jesus said, *The devil...speaketh a lie."* Again, the Greek structure says, *"the devil speaks "the lie."* What is *"the lie?"* One facet of it is speaking from ones own self. The other facet is creature worship. This encompasses denying the Father and the Son by causing worship of ones own self.

47

Remember the one who denies the Father and the Son is an antichrist, and one facet of antichrist is the *"many false prophets."*

CREATURE WORSHIP

Revelation 13:4, NIV:
*Men **worshiped the dragon** because he had given authority to the beast, and they also **worshiped the beast** and asked, "Who is like the beast? Who can make war against him?"*

In the verse above men worshipped the dragon and the beast. This is most detestable to God. You may say, "Why is that?" The depth of the statement above is in the spirit. The statement in the verse above is synonymous with homosexuality/lesbianism—now do not close the book. I am not against homosexual and lesbians (I Corinthians 6:9-11). In the verse above, we see the created beings (men) worshiping the created beasts (the dragon and the beast). What does this have to do with homosexuality? *Homo is the Greek word for "same." Sexuality is: the gender of a species.*

Therefore, "same sex" means homo-sexuality/ lesbianism. Worship means, to kiss (Vines). It is a very intimate word. Understand the mystery. Creature worshipping creature is the same as men having sexual relations men or women having sexual relations with women (Romans 1:26). All created things are of the same *gender* in this sense: they are *"created things."* The Creator is in a class by Himself (Isaiah 44:8). He is

48

The Creator. Therefore, created things worshiping created things are just like homosexual acts. Do you understand this?

Creatures (mankind, angels, animals) were created to worship the **Creator—God**—not creatures worshiping creatures. And for those who do not believe there is the living God, they are lying. God shows Himself to every human (Romans 1:28).

I remember as a young boy in Jamaica, West Indies, I was walking through the walkway a jot pass the gate. At that moment it appears that I was transfixed between heaven and earth; and I looked up and said, "Surely there must be a God." That was God revealing Himself to me at a young age. I was not brought up in Church; however, I realized there must be a Creator. His name is Jesus. God reveals Himself **in** every creature (Romans 10:18). However, mankind still insists on creature worship.

This creature worship is the lie the Devil fathered. The Devil fathered the concept of man and angels (created beings) worshiping him, his idols (images of created things) and animals (created things), **instead of God (the Creator).** He spoke of his own self (John 8:44). He spoke of his own worship (Luke 4:6-8). He caused other created things—angels and men—to kiss him instead of the Christ.

Romans 1:25, NIV:
*They exchanged the truth of God for **a lie (lit; the lie),** and worshiped and served **created things** rather than the Creator—who is forever praised. Amen.*

Paul said that anyone who *"exchanged the truth of God for the lie"* is the same as worshiping and serving the *"created things"* rather than the *"Creator."* *"22 Although they claimed to be wise, they became fools 23and* **exchanged** *the glory of the immortal God for* **images made to look like** *mortal* **man** *and* **birds** *and* **animals** *and* **reptiles"** (Romans 1:22-23). The lie, according to Romans 1:25 quoted above, is when the created things (mankind/angels) worship other created things (each other), which range from excessive love of animals to worshipping human body parts more than the Living God. In Revelation 13 the people worshipped the *"dragon"*—a *"reptile"* and the *"beast"*— a four footed animal which points to man and his government systems that is anti-God (See Daniel 7). In Revelation 13, they worshipped the *"image of the beast",* which in the words of Romans 1:23, is *"images made to look like ... animals."*

As you can see, Revelation 13 lines up with Romans 1:23 perfectly, it does not stop there. Paul said God allowed these people to do in the natural what they were doing in the spirit. Creature was worshiping creature of the same specie—the class of created things. Therefore, he allowed men to have anal sex with men and women, and women having sexual relations with women *"for the degrading of their bodies with one another"* (Romans 1:24, last part). ***Note: I will not take the time in this book to teach in detail about the reprobation of anal sex that is so popular in many*** *countries, except to say, that the Old Testament teach that adultery also causes the spread of anal sex.*

Therefore in God's sight, whenever a person worships the creation—whales, dogs, birds, women/men body parts in magazines, athletes, idolized singers, pastor worship, self-worship, etc—it is just like homosexuals caught in the act. In fact, most of the people who do these things are either homosexuals, lesbians, bisexual or sexually perverted. Do a little research and you will see that the statement I just made is true! Creature worshiping creature is dirty in God's sight. *Most animals are made to eat* (Genesis 9:2-3; I Corinthians 6:13), *not to be worshiped.* This does not mean that we abuse animals. We are instructed to take care of our animals (Proverb 12:10, NIV). **The question is though: "Can the homosexuals, lesbians and bisexuals receive deliverance?" Yes! Some will be saved.**

I Corinthians 6:9-11, NIV:
[9] *Do you not know that the wicked will not inherit the kingdom of God? Do not be deceived: Neither the sexually immoral nor idolaters nor adulterers nor male prostitutes nor* **homosexual offenders** [10] *nor thieves nor the greedy nor drunkards nor slanderers nor swindlers will inherit the kingdom of God.* [11] **And that is what some of you were.** *But you were washed, you were sanctified, you were justified in the name of the Lord Jesus Christ and by the Spirit of our God.*

51

Paul said, *"And that is what some of you were."* Therefore, those who *"are homosexual offenders,"* the ones who worship the creatures—whales, cats, dogs, birds, self, and other humans instead of God can be saved. In the Name of the Lord Jesus Christ and by the Spirit of God they can be washed, sanctified and justified. Yes! Yes! Yes! The same Christ that they deny is the same Christ that is extending His arm to forgive them.

In conclusion, do not be caught dead—literally—worshiping the creature. The penalty for that crime is eternal torment with fire and brimstone (Revelation 14:10-11). Revelation 17 said that those whose names are not written in the book of life will be the ones who worship the beast—a creature. Are you worshipping beasts—four footed, or two footed men and women? Stop! It is the homosexual spirits of Satan, the beast and the false prophets that are the fathers of these acts. False prophets, the antichrists, will deny the Christ. They will cause worship of themselves.

It is easy as a man or woman of God to allow people to worship him/her. But you must stop it. If you do not stop it (Revelation 22:8-9, Acts 10:25-26, Acts 14:9-15) homosexuality is around the corner waiting for you. Let us get it clear, we should respect the man and woman of God (I Thessalonians 5:12-13), but we should never worship fallen mankind in any form. There is a difference between respect and worship. False prophets, like Satan, want to steel God's kiss. Yet, true prophets will receive respect out of worship to their God (I Samuel 16:4). Why? They do not speak from their own heart or private interpretation. They do not do the lie. They do not deny the Father and the Son. I conclude:

I John 2:22-23, NIV:
[22] Who is the liar? It is the man who denies that Jesus is the Christ. Such a man is the antichrist—he denies the Father and the Son. [23] No one who denies the Son has the Father; whoever acknowledges the Son has the Father also.

CHAPTER 4
MANY FALSE PROPHETS

Revelation 16:13, NIV:
*Then I saw three **evil spirits** that looked like frogs; they came out of the mouth of the dragon, out of the mouth of the beast and **out of the mouth of the false prophet.***

I John 4:1, NIV:
*[1]Dear friends, do not believe every **spirit,** but test the spirits to see whether they are from God, because **many false prophets** have gone out into the world. [2]This is how you can recognize the Spirit of God: Every spirit that acknowledges that Jesus Christ has come in the flesh is from God, [3] but every spirit that does not acknowledge Jesus is not from God. This is the **spirit of the antichrist,** which you have heard is coming and even now is already in the world.*

False prophets manifest themselves in *"many"* forms. Thus, there are *"many false prophets."* This chapter will deal with the many **forms** the false prophet spirit manifest itself. An important aspect to remember is that behind the *"many false prophets"* is **"one spirit."** The **spirit of antichrist** has the ability to reproduce or expand it self to cover *"many false prophets."*

In Revelation 16:13 cited above, we see that the "rebellious three" could multiply themselves by releasing evil—lit; unclean—spirits out of their mouths.

The false prophet is included in the number above. If a false prophet, prophesy over a person, he is releasing a frog spirit on that individual. In the land of Egypt, Moses multiplied the frogs in Egypt as a judgment. God (Moses in type—Exodus 7:1) is allowing a spirit like a frog to leave the false prophet's mouth to judge by deception (II Thessalonians 2:9-11). The reason why there is continuity among the false prophets is because there is one lying spirit among them.

ONE LYING SPIRIT IN THE MANY MOUTHS

II Chronicles 18:22, NIV:
*"So now the LORD has put **a lying spirit** in the **mouths** of these prophets of yours. The LORD has decreed disaster for you."*

In the verse above the scripture is plain. *"A"* (singular) lying spirit was in the *"mouths"* (plural) of the prophets (plural). In fact, this one lying spirit was in the ***"mouths"*** (Revelation 16:13) of *"four hundred"* (400) false prophets (II Chronicles 18:5). Be careful about *"the many false prophets"* bearing witness with each other. All of the false prophets that prophesied to Jehoshaphat all said the **same** false words. *"Go,"* **they** answered, *"for God will give it into the king's hand"* (II Chronicles 18:5). They also said, *"Attack Ramoth Gilead and be victorious,"* **they** said, *"for the LORD will give it into the king's hand"* (II Chronicles 18:11). They even used the name of the Lord. But we know from verse 22 that they prophesied by a lying spirit.

The true prophet was contrary to the many false prophets. In fact, King Ahab hated this true prophet. This is indicative to all true prophets. True prophets are hated. Micaiah told the truth and was hated for it. **Principle:** *A true prophet is usually opposite the voice of the majority.* Listen to the scripture:

II Chronicles 18:17-22, NIV:
16 Then Micaiah answered, "I saw all Israel scattered on the hills like sheep without a shepherd, and the LORD said, 'These people have no master. Let each one go home in peace."

17 The king of Israel said to Jehoshaphat, "Didn't I tell you that he never prophesies anything good about me, but only bad?"

18 Micaiah continued, "Therefore hear the word of the LORD: I saw the LORD sitting on his throne with all the host of heaven standing on his right and on his left.

*19 **And the LORD said, 'Who will entice** Ahab king of Israel into attacking Ramoth Gilead and **going to his death there?'** "One suggested this, and another that.*

20 Finally, a spirit came forward, stood before the LORD and said, 'I will entice him.' "'By what means?' the LORD asked.

21 'I will go and be a lying spirit in the mouths of all his prophets,' he said. "'You will succeed in enticing him,' said the LORD. 'Go and do it.'

22 "So now the LORD has put a lying spirit in the mouths of these prophets of yours. The LORD has decreed disaster for you."

It was a heavy word—death to the rebellious king—but Micaiah revealed the truth. In the same manner, this book is telling the truth concerning false prophets, false shepherds, false elders, wizards, witches, etc. The false prophets were prophesying *"success"* in a war that God obviously did not sanction for Ahab's benefit (II Chronicles 18:12-19). There is *"death"* in this apparent *"success."* In verse 19 Micaiah declared, *"And the LORD said, who will entice Ahab.... to **his death** there." **Principle**: When false prophets prophesy success, there is really "death" in the end.*

"I see a house," they say but there might be death (overwhelming debt) in that house if it is attained out of season. I see you with a "new" husband. That "new" husband may be a pseudo saint. These statements may be extreme, however, they are true. I would like to say at this point, false prophets do not negate the work and words of the true prophets of God (Ephesians 4:11; Acts 11:27-30). Prophets from God do prophesy encouraging things. *"Judas and Silas, who themselves were **prophets**, said **much** to encourage and strengthen the brothers"* (Acts 15:32).

We have learned so far that *"one"* lying spirit can multiply among those who are false. This is the same thing that the Apostle John said. He taught that *"the spirit of antichrist"* exists among the *"many false prophets."* They all have one message, **"worldly** success" without a consecrated lifestyle.

The *"viewpoint"* of the world is to have success from their point-of-view, not God's. Ahab and his wife Jezebel were full of witchcraft, covetousness and murder. Yet, they wanted a word of *"success"* from God. The viewpoint of the "worldly church" is: to use/do witchcraft, sorcery, magic, etc, and then ask God for *"success"* like Ahab did. The spirit of antichrist speaks from the *"viewpoint of the world."*

WORLDLY VIEWPOINT

I John 4:1, NIV:
[1]Dear friends, do not believe every **spirit,** *but test the spirits to see whether they are from God, because* **many false prophets** *have gone out into the world.*

I John 4:3, NIV:
[3] but every spirit that does not acknowledge Jesus is not from God. This is the **spirit of the antichrist,** *which you have heard is coming and even now is already in the world.*

1 John 4:5, NIV
[5]They are from the world and therefore speak from the **viewpoint of the world,** *and the world listens to them.*

The spirit (singular) of antichrist is the one among the *"many false prophets"* and they have a worldly point-of-view. What is the purpose of knowing this? Do not be carried away with every wind of the worldly doctrine of false prophets that *"bear witness"* with the worldly attitudes of the lust of the flesh, lust of the eyes and the pride of life (I John 2:15-16, KJV; I Timothy 6:3-10, NIV). The voice of the majority saying the same thing does not mean it is from God. Allow me to give you some understanding.

All of the false prophets of II Chronicles 18 were all bearing witness to each other. They **all** were saying *"success."* The reason is because they all spoke from the **one** evil spirit. Today, the one spirit of antichrist is among the *"many false prophets."* In II Chronicles their words were <u>anti-God's</u> point-of-view. In the New Testament they are called <u>antichrists.</u> Their point-of-view is worldly. All the false prophets were saying the same words which were contrary to God until Micaiah showed up.

Micaiah means "the one who is like God." In this Dark Age, the "Micaiahs" will be contrary to those who depend on the deceptive witness of each other to please the kings—ungodly people of positions in the Church and the world. One of the false prophets' name is "Zedekiah son of Kenaanah." Zedekiah means right of Jah. Kenaanah is defined as humiliated.

This means that among the false prophets there is a witness of false—outward—**humility** and they feel they have the **"right"** of God to say, "The Lord is saying." But the truth is: there is an evil spirit of antichrist in their mouth and heart. In their private lives, they are "worldly"—lust of the flesh, lust of the eyes and the pride of life (I John 2:16, KJV). Remember, when there are the *"many"* witnesses it does not necessarily mean God is in it. I am going to tell you the truth concerning this age with respect to the four hundred (400) false prophets in II Chronicles 18 who may be the left over from the 850 false prophets per I

Kings 18:40. These were the prophets of Baal that Elijah by the word of the Lord challenged.

In this age for every 400-850 prophets there is only one (1) "who is like God" (Micaiah or Elijah). Percentage wise, this is 0.12%-0.25%. Note: Not twelve to twenty five percents, but **point** twelve percent to **point** twenty five percent. Elijah was one among eight hundred and fifty. Micaiah was one among four hundred. In other words, out of every 451-851 prophets **who say** they are speaking from God only one (1) is true. The other 400-850 is not from God, and they will *"slap"* the faces of some of the true prophets who expose them (II Chronicles 18:23). It does not stop there though.

Those who are walking in the spirit of Elijah will slay the false prophets of this age with the words of God (I Kings 18:40 with Revelation 11:5). As stated above, there is a spirit of antichrist that is prophesying worldly *"success"* without living a clean life before the Lord, and they are the majority. I John 4: 5-6 teaches that the false prophets through the spirit of antichrist *"speak from the **viewpoint** of the world.... This is how we recognize the Spirit of truth and the **spirit of falsehood.**"*

I John 2:15-16, NIV:

*15 Do not love the world or anything in the world. If anyone **loves the world, the love of the Father is not in him.** 16 For everything in the **world**—the **cravings of sinful man,** the **lust of his eyes** and the **boasting of what he has and does**—comes not from the Father but from the **world.***

Be watchful in this age. There are many false children who claim they are children of Jesus, but they are children of the world. They use secret arts of hell (Isaiah 57:3; 57:9, KJV) and pretend to be of Jesus. Did you notice that palm readers house all have a cross on it? Some even use the name of Jesus (compare Matthews 7:22) as they use witchcraft and sorcery. *"The love of the father is not in them."* They have stealthy crept into the lives of people—saved and unsaved—and claim to be of God. The fact of the matter is they are magicians. In today's terms they are called palm readers, witches, warlocks, sorcerers, psychics, etc. One of the many forms that false prophets will be displayed as is: *"Bar-Jesus."*

BAR JESUS

Acts 13:6, NIV:
*They traveled through the whole island until they came to Paphos. There they met **a Jewish sorcerer** and **false prophet** named **Bar-Jesus** ...*

Paul and Barnabas were released for apostolic work. The first thing they encountered on their mission was a false prophet. **Principle**: *Typically, the first oppositions newly sent apostles and prophets will encounter are witches.* They will come and sit in your church and try to create disruption in the spirit which spills over in the natural. If the man of God does not deal with that/those witchcraft/witches right of way, he

61

will always have trouble in that area. Let us see how Paul dealt with it. I will begin with the phrase *"Bar-Jesus."*

"Bar-Jesus" means "son of Jesus." This *"sorcerer"* was also a *"Jew."* This same so-called *"son of Jesus,"* this same *"Jew"* is also called a *"false prophet."* This is easy to follow so far, right? There are principles in this event that may be applied to this age. Let us explore them. First, I will explicate the sorcerer being called *"son of Jesus."* Our Lord Jesus said, *"For many will come in my name"* (Matthew 24:5).

This means that *"many"* false ones will come using the *"name"* of Jesus. False prophets of the world will say they are of Jesus. How do they "say" this? A good example of this is they will use the cross as a sign on their palm reading houses. They will use the name of Jesus in pronouncing their spells. It goes further.

Some of the false sons of Jesus are pastors. I met a lady years ago that was a "pastor." I later found out that she read palms and performed divination. This is just the tip. There are so-called pastors who seek words from mediums like King Saul did (I Samuel 28). There are some so-called preachers who get their words from mediums and they preach it in their pulpit on Sundays. The result of their folly will be death like Saul. How do you recognize these false prophets? We will see in a moment.

The next thing is that the false prophet is called a *"Jew."* This goes back to what Jesus said about false prophets coming in sheep's clothing. There are false prophets who claim to be Jews (Christians). They claim to be circumcised inwardly.

Romans 2:28-29, KJV:
[28] *For he is not a Jew, which is one outwardly; neither is that circumcision, which is outward in the flesh:* [29] *But he is a Jew, which is one **inwardly;** and circumcision is that of the heart, in the spirit, and not in the letter; whose praise is not of men, but of God.*

The fact of the matter is that false prophets acknowledgement of being a believer is outward. That is, they pretend to be saved—circumcised inwardly (Romans 2:29 with Colossians 2:11)—but their heart is filled with the *"deceit and trickery"* (Acts 8:10-22). The purpose of the spirit of the false prophet's trickery and deceit is to turn people from faith in Jesus. The false prophet that Paul and Barnabas encountered was trying to turn a man from the faith.

Acts 13:6-8, NIV:
[6] *They traveled through the whole island until they came to Paphos. There they met a Jewish sorcerer and false prophet named Bar-Jesus,* [7] *who was an attendant of the proconsul, Sergius Paulus. The proconsul, an intelligent man, sent for Barnabas and Saul because he wanted to hear the word of God.* [8] *But Elymas the sorcerer (for that is what his name means) **opposed** them and tried to **turn** the proconsul from **the faith.***

The word warlock, a male witch, means, "To break faith." The reason why faith is so hard to attain in some Churches is because warlocks are sitting in Church, including the pulpit, opposing everything that is of faith. The spirit of the false prophet like a frog is leaping about in some circles. This is the attitude that Paul and Barnabas encountered. The sorcerer *"opposed them and tried to **turn** the proconsul from **the faith.**"* If there is a temptation to turn from the faith and call the psychic hotline, to see palm readers, to do necromancy, then a warlock spirit is present.

That frog spirit is trying to break your faith in Jesus. The sign of this spirit is: no prayer life, no study life, no fasting life, and no faith life. There is a judgment for these false prophets who turn people from the faith of Jesus Christ. God is raising apostles and prophets who will judge the false ones with swiftness and severity. This is the age when God is raising up Judges— prophetic apostles and apostolic prophets.

Acts 13:9-12, NIV:
*[9] Then Saul, who was also called Paul, filled with the Holy Spirit, looked straight at Elymas and said, [10] "You are a child of the devil and an enemy of everything that is right! You are full of all kinds of deceit and trickery. Will you never stop perverting the right ways of the Lord? [11] Now **the hand of the Lord is against you.** You are going to be **blind,** and for a time you will be unable to see the light of the sun." **Immediately** mist and darkness came over him, and he groped about, seeking someone to lead him by the hand. [12] When the proconsul*

saw what had happened, he believed, for he was amazed at the teaching about the Lord.

Did you hear that? The Holy Spirit filled Paul. Paul was not terrified—Jeremiah 1:17—he *"looked straight at Elymas and said, "The hand of the Lord is against you. You are going to be blind...."* God is establishing prophets and apostles who will look at false prophets with the wrong spirit straight in the eyes and judge the evil. How will this judgment manifest? *"The hand of the Lord"* will be *"against"* them and the Lord will do his judgment *"immediately."* The result of the judgment is that people will *"believe."* They will fear the Lord and get "right" real quick. *"When **the proconsul** saw what had happened, **he believed,** for he was amazed at the teaching about the Lord"* (Acts 13:12).

In conclusion of this chapter, I will discuss the controversial matter of money. One of the marks of false prophets is the merchandising of the saints. I will exegete this with balance.

EMPORIUM

Revelation 13:16-17, NIV:
[16] *He also forced everyone, small and great, rich and poor, free and slave, to receive a mark on his right hand or on his forehead,* [17] ***so that no one could buy or sell unless he had the mark,*** *which is the name of the beast or the number of his name.*

II Peter 2:1-3, NIV:

*1 But there were also **false prophets** among the people, just as there will be **false teachers** among you. They will secretly introduce destructive heresies, even denying the sovereign Lord who bought them—bringing swift destruction on themselves. 2 Many will follow their shameful ways and will bring the way of truth into disrepute. 3 In their greed these teachers will **exploit** you with stories they have made up. Their condemnation has long been hanging over them, and their destruction has not been sleeping.*

False prophets will *"exploit"* the saints. *"Exploit"* in the Greek is "emporeuomai"—this is where we get our English word emporium. It is translated in the King James as **"buy and sell"** and **"merchandise."** The New International Version also translates it as **"carry on business."** In Revelation 13:17 we learn that **buying and selling** involves the **mark** of the beast. Mark is defined as "character" from the Greek "charagma" (see Volume 1 and 2).

Therefore, if false prophets *"merchandise,"* or *"buy and sell,"* or *"carry on business"* in the church, it is because they have the character (mark) of the beast in their minds or foreheads (Revelation 13:16). The Church has become a market place for false prophets. They will not come to your Church unless there is a *"price."* They have reduced the Church to a *"business."* The "Dove", Holy Spirit's anointing, now has a price in the Church (John 2:16 with Luke 3:22).

Micah 3:9-11, NIV:

^{9} *Hear this, you leaders of the house of Jacob, you rulers of the house of Israel, who despise justice and distort all that is right;* ^{10} *who build Zion with bloodshed, and Jerusalem with wickedness.* ^{11} *Her leaders judge for a* **bribe,** *her priests teach for **a price,** and her prophets tell fortunes **for money. Yet they lean upon the LORD and say, "Is not the LORD among us?** No disaster will come upon us."*

God is troubled over what is going on in *"Zion"*—the Church (Hebrews 12:22). Listen: *"Her **leaders** judge for a **bribe,** her **priests teach** for **a price,** and her **prophets** tell fortunes **for money."** * It does not stop there. The have the nerve to say, "Isn't this an anointed service. In the words of Micah, *"they lean upon the LORD and say, "Is not the LORD among us?"* The Lord is **not** among them. It is not an anointed service. According to Revelation 13 they have the mark of the beast; because they are merchandising God's people. I have been in Churches where if you do not give a certain amount to the preacher, they make you feel small.

I have been in Church services where the length of prophesies depended on how much a person gave. The $1000 line got long prophesies. The $25 line received short prophesies. I have seen a so-called preacher stop the meeting to "sell" **his** book, and said the meeting would not go on until someone buys **his** book. He then made **"war"** on those who did not have the money to buy his book by calling them "poor." Do you know that the false prophets in Micah's days did the same thing? They made *"war"* on those who did not *"feed"* them.

Micah 3:5, NIV:
*This is what the LORD says: As for **the prophets** who lead my people astray, **if one feeds them, they proclaim 'peace'**; if he does not, they prepare to **wage war** against him.*

This describes the false prophets of today. If you do not *"feed"* them with the amount of money they ask for, prepare for war. They will tear you down. They will say you will not have "peace," and try to use Malachi 3 to curse you. Cursing God's people is false doctrine. Did you know that Jesus Christ *"redeemed us from the curse of the law"* (Galatians 3:13)? There is a **change** of the priesthood from *"law"*—which involves curses—to *"life"*— which involves *"blessings." "For when there is a **change** of the priesthood, there must also be a **change** of the law"* (Hebrews 7:12).

The law of cursing has been changed to the law of the Spirit of life which blesses (Romans 8:1-2, Hebrews 7:16). Melchizedek *"blessed"* Abraham **before** Abraham *"tithed"* to him (Genesis 14: 18-20), Refer to my book *"The Torah (Principle) of Giving"*). The priesthood of Jesus should bless the people with life and the people will tithe. However, in Micah 3:10, the false prophets used *"wickedness"* to *"build"* Zion. God is going to expose this wicked building. He shall expose everything down to the foundation.

In Ezekiel 13, God came against the false prophets. He said that they built a *"flimsy wall"* with their false prophesies. The judgment was to tear down what was built upon wickedness. *"I will tear down the wall you have covered with whitewash and will level it to the ground so that **its foundation will be laid bare.** When it falls, you will be destroyed in it; and you will know that I am the LORD"* (Ezekiel 13:14).

God is going to expose the *"foundation"* of the false prophets. They call themselves sons of Jesus. But they are not. Jesus is the true foundation (I Corinthians 3:11). Therefore when God said the *"foundation will be laid bare,"* He means that he will expose the heart of these false prophets that all may see that there is no Jesus in their lives. They have built Zion on the *"evil"* of the love of money. Their foundation is money, not Jesus. It is more excellent to preach the word of God for free. There is reward in preaching the gospel for free.

I Corinthians 9:18, NIV:
*What then is my **reward**? Just this: that in preaching the gospel I may offer it **free of charge**, and so not make use of my rights in preaching it.*

The reward of preaching the gospel is to offer it freely. It should give us pleasure to teach *"free of charge."* We do not have to always *"make use"* of our *"rights in preaching"* the gospel. Now the balance to this is that the true Believer **must** give to the true man of God. It is their duty. They owe it to us. However, the man of God must not abuse this *"right"* by merchandising the people of God.

Romans 15:25-27, NIV:
[25] Now, however, I am on my way to Jerusalem in the service of the saints there.[26] For Macedonia and Achaia were pleased to make a contribution for the poor among the saints in Jerusalem. [27] They were pleased to do it, and indeed they owe it to them. For if the Gentiles have shared in the Jews' spiritual blessings, they owe it to the Jews to share with them their material blessings.

The principle in the scripture above is that if some partake of a spiritual blessing, they *"owe it"* to give *"material blessings."* Therefore, when the men of God teach the Church *"spiritual"* words, then the recipient should give their *"material blessings."* The King James Version translates it as *"their duty"* (Romans 15:27) to do this service.

I Corinthians 9:11, NJV:
*If we have sown **spiritual seed** among you, is it too much if we reap a material harvest from you?*

The Church must keep the verse above in mind for those who are of the Truth. The true men of God must eat (I Corinthians 9:7-10) and they should also reap. But there is a qualification. The prophets of God must **"sow spiritual seed"** which according to Peter is the word of God (I Peter 1:23-25). If you are sowing **carnality,** then you should not get paid. In other words if you are lazy and do not pray, study and fast to receive a word from God you should not get paid. However, the very ones who are lazy and do not seek God pressure the Church to support their lazy attitude.

We must not allow the Church of the living God to become a market place, where leaders are using sales tactics and sale pressures to merchandise the Church of the living God. The true leader must exercise self-control and not put a price on the gospel. Paul made a statement concerning money and self-control. Men of God quote it, but they do not understand it. If you do not believe me read the text again and see the logical link.

I Corinthians 9:27, NIV:
*No, **I beat my body and make it my slave so** that after I have preached to others, I myself will not be disqualified for the prize.*

In conclusion of this chapter, Paul made the statement above with respect to preaching the gospel without charge (Read I Corinthians 9:1-21). There are many false prophets in the land. They are *"disqualified for the prize."* **They have not disciplined their bodies not to always ask for money.** Yes! It is a lack of discipline in the body that caused false prophets to merchandise the people of God.

It takes self-discipline not to ask for money and trust in God for supplies as he moves on the heart of the saints to give. The false prophets who travel for the sake of money and those not disciplined enough to refrain from pressuring the Saints for money will be *"disqualified."* God will expose their foundation.

Next, we take a look at the true prophets of God. We will see how they function in a distinct manner from the many false prophets in the world today. We will conclude with a prophet's interpretation.

CHAPTER 5
A PROPHET'S INTERPRETATION

Revelation 5:1-5, NIV:
*[1] Then I saw in the right hand of him who sat on the throne a scroll with writing on both sides and **sealed with seven seals.** [2] And I saw a mighty angel proclaiming in a loud voice, "Who is worthy to break the seals and open the scroll?" [3] But no one in heaven or on earth or under the earth could open the scroll or even look inside it. [4] I wept and wept because no one was found who was worthy to open the scroll or look inside. [5] Then one of the elders said to me, "Do not weep! **See, the Lion of the tribe of Judah, the Root of David, has triumphed. He is able to open the scroll and its seven seals."***

If something is sealed from understanding, it will take a true prophet to open, or interpret the sayings of the living God. We have heard about the false ones in this manuscript, however, that do not negate the fact that there are indeed true prophets that exist today. The whole church is quick to say there are false prophets. However, they are not "quick" or willing to say there are true prophets who understand the mystery of God (Revelation 10:7; Ephesians 3:1-6, etc.). The apostles' and prophets' interpretations are necessary. In fact, in

73

this age, the mystery of His will for this generation will only be known through the apostles and prophets (Ephesians 3). Understand this: the prophets of Jesus must receive their interpretation from *"The Prophet."* His name—nature, character and authority—is Lamblike.

In Revelation 5 John, an apostle, could not understand what was written in the book in God's hand. The Lamb of God—Jesus, the Prophet, had to *"open the scroll"* for him. In this last chapter we will learn about "the Prophet's interpretation" through His apostles and prophets.

APOSTLES AND PROPHETS UNTIL...

Ephesians 4:11-13, NIV
*[11] It was he who gave some to be **apostles,** some to be **prophets,** some to be evangelists, and some to be pastors and teachers, [12] to prepare God's people for works of service, so that the body of Christ may be built up [14] until we all reach unity in the faith and in the knowledge of the Son of God and become mature, attaining to the whole measure of the fullness of Christ.*

The reason why "all" prophets are labeled false today is because a lot of "pastors" do not believe in the prophet's authority (Matthew 21:23-24). They (some pastors) are teaching lies when they say true prophets do not exists today. They go as far as forbidding the prophetic (Jeremiah 11:21; Amos 2:12; Amos 7:13-17; I Thessalonians 5:20). If pastors exist today so do prophets and apostles. The same God who gave pastors is the One who gave apostles and prophets. Allow me to explain.

Ephesians 4:11-13, NIV:
[11] *It was **he who gave some to be apostles**, some to be prophets, some to be evangelists, and some to be pastors and teachers,* [12] *to prepare God's people for works of service, so that the body of Christ may be built up* [13] **until** *we all reach unity in the faith and in the knowledge of the Son of God and become mature, attaining to the whole measure of the fullness of Christ.*

"It was he [Jesus] who gave some to be apostles, some to be prophets... and some to be pastors and teachers." Jesus gave these gifts. The Greek text for the first part of the phrase reads: "Kaí (And) autos (He) édooken (gave) toús (the) **mén (in fact)** apostólous (apostles)..." This reads "And he gave **in fact** the apostles." "**Mén**" according to Strong's Concordance is defined as: "a primary particle; properly, indicative of *affirmation or concession (in fact);* usually followed by a *contrasted* clause with NT:*1161 (this* one, the *former,* etc)." Therefore apostles and prophets existence is an **"affirmation"** of **"fact."**

In fact, He gave them **"until." "Until we all reach unity in the faith..."** Did **"all"** the Church "*reach unity in the faith* **and** *in the knowledge of the son of God",* etc? Obviously the answer is no! Listen now.

Pastors are needed to help the church "*reach unity.*" **Teachers** are needed to help the church "*reach* *unity."* **Evangelists** are needed to help the church *"reach unity."* **Prophets**—yes prophets—are needed to help the church *"reach unity."* And last but not least, **Apostles** are needed to help the church *"reach unity."* These gifts are given *"until."* *"Until"* is a "time" word. They are given until *"all"* the Church **attain** *"to the whole measure of the fullness of Christ."* I repeat, if pastors, teachers and evangelists exist today, then by logic according to Ephesians 4:11-13, apostles and prophets exist today, *"in fact."* The Church is so backwards. We are created with five fingers. If one is missing, it becomes difficult to use the hand properly. This is the same with the five-fold gifts.

The Church has received the false prophets and rejected the true prophets. The reason why there are so many false ones in the Church is because the true prophets are not allowed to function properly. A Church will never mature unless they allow all five gifts to minister to the body. False prophets will not be eradicated without the function of true prophets (Jeremiah 28:16-17).

A car is made up of many components. If you remove the tires the car will not be able to go forward without the wheel. This is the same principle with apostles and prophets. Because they are missing from the body, the body will not go forward—mature. If a part is missing there will be deformity. If the apostles and prophets are missing, the body will be deformed. In fact, I am not so sure that people who have a *deformed hand—one finger, which is a lone pastor*—can draw near to offer food to his God. **Note: I am referring to a**

spiritual principle, not people who are maimed physically.

Leviticus 21:16-18, NIV:
[16] *The LORD said to Moses,* [17] *"Say to Aaron: 'For the generations to come none of your descendants who has a **defect may come near to offer the food of his God.*** [18] ***No man who has any defect may come near:** no man who is blind or lame, disfigured or **deformed...**"*

This is plain enough. God is always interested in a *"whole"* man. Paul said, *"May God himself, the God of peace, sanctify you **through and through**. May your **whole** spirit, soul and body be kept blameless at the coming of our Lord Jesus Christ"* (I Thessalonians 5:23, NIV). This is that *"perfect man"* that the apostles and prophets will aid in perfecting the Church through the Spirit of Jesus Christ. Every part of the body is important. We *"need"* every part.

I Corinthians 12:21, NIV:
*"The eye cannot say to the hand, **"I don't need you!"** And the head cannot say to the feet, **"I don't need you!"***

I Corinthians 12:27-28, NIV:
[27] *Now you are the body of Christ, and **each one of you** is a **part** of it.* [28] *And in the church God has appointed first of all apostles, second prophets, third teachers, then workers of miracles, also those having gifts of healing, those able to help others, those with gifts of*

77

administration, and those speaking in different kinds of tongues.

The **parts** of the *"body"* are *"**apostles**, second **prophets**, third **teachers**, then **workers of miracles**, also those having **gifts of healing**, **those able to help others**, those with gifts of **administration**, and those speaking in **different kinds of tongues**,"* etc. All the pastors who decide to cut out the apostles and prophets; let them also cut themselves out. Let them say, "I will not recognize pastors anymore in the Church." Let us go a little further, let a Church say they do not need their pastor anymore. That pastor would be hurt; and the Church would go about without pastoral care. The same is true for apostles and prophets. The Church will lack apostolic knowledge and the prophetic scope. For example, the Church will lack sight and timing without the prophets and apostles, because prophets "see" and apostles "know."

It is not right for pastors to reject a part—apostles and prophets—of themselves. What if you decide to cut your thumb off? Will you be able to **grasp** an object properly? The answer is no! The same is true for the apostles and prophets. Most of the church of today cannot "grasp" certain truth because **their** pastors, **their** evangelists and **their** teachers have rejected the prophetic and apostolic gifts. Do not be like the carnal Corinthians and say, *"I don't need you!"* The Lord is saying, "We need each other."

If you reject prophets today, you reject Jesus— Deuteronomy 18:15, John 4:19; 4:44; 6:14, 7:40, 9:17—

because Jesus is *"The Prophet." The crowds answered, "This is Jesus, the prophet from Nazareth in Galilee"* (Matthew 21:11, NIV). Sometimes it is only the crowds of people who are following Jesus who acknowledge true prophets. The leaders are too insecure and jealous to acknowledge apostles and prophets (Matthew 27:18; Acts 13:45).

If you reject apostles then you reject Jesus because, He is *"the Apostle." "Therefore, holy brothers, who share in the heavenly calling, fix your thoughts on Jesus, the apostle and high priest whom we confess" (Hebrews 3:1).* This same Apostle and Prophet gave apostles and prophets. In fact he divided Himself into *"many parts"* (I Corinthians 12:12).

He is The Apostle—He gave some to be apostles. He is The Prophet—He gave some to be prophets. He is The Evangelists—He gave some to be evangelists. He is The Good Shepherd—He gave some to be shepherds. Finally He is the Rabbi—He gave some to be teachers. Let the church embrace the rest of her *"many parts"*— apostolic and prophetic ministries. The apostles and prophets will cause the Church and the unsaved to understand the mysteries of God.

THE UNINTERPRETABLE

Genesis 41:1, NIV:
When two full years had passed, Pharaoh had a dream: He was standing by the Nile ...

Genesis 41:15, NIV:
Pharaoh said to Joseph, "I had a dream, and no one can interpret it. But I have heard it said of you that when you hear a dream you can interpret it."

Genesis 41:16, NIV:
"I cannot do it," Joseph replied to Pharaoh, "but God will give Pharaoh the answer he desires."

Pharaoh had a dream *"when two full years had passed"* (Genesis 41:1). The Hebrew reads, **"And it was at the end of two years of days that Pharaoh was dreaming."** This is very significant prophetically. The "year-day" principle is seen in this verse. The Church is "two years of days" from Jesus. The Apostle Peter in II Peter 3:8 said, *"But do not forget this one thing, dear friends:* **With** *the Lord a day is like a thousand years, and a thousand years are like a day."* Did you hear that? A thousand years *"with (lit.; near)"* the Lord is like one day; and one day is like a thousand years.

With respect to Jesus, Pharaoh's year-day dream points to the end of the two thousand years of days starting from Jesus' death burial and resurrection until approximately 2033. Do you agree that 2001 AD is approximately two thousand years from Jesus death burial and resurrection? Therefore, we are approximately two days (2000) from Jesus—*"the last Adam"* (I Corinthians 15:45)—and close to the end of 6 days—6000 years from *"the first Adam"* (I Corinthians 12:12). Can you see this? Thus, a principle may be gained from the "timing" of the dream God gave Pharaoh.

At the end of two years of days (2000 years) from Jesus, God is causing the Pharaohs—all who claim to be leaders, those ranging from drug dealers to presidents—to dream. Another way of saying this is: This is the season when the Father is speaking about the future to all classes of people that includes, but are not limited to leaders, rich, poor, bond, and free. And just like Pharaoh, they are people who use the evil of "magicians," and "wise men" to try to interpret their dreams. There is only one catch. Magicians, palm-readers, etc. cannot interpret a dream that really comes from God. It will take apostolic and prophetic interpretation.

Genesis 41:8, NIV:
*In the morning his **mind** was troubled, so he sent for all the **magicians** and wise men of Egypt. Pharaoh told them his dreams, **but no one could interpret** them for him.*

His mind (lit; spirit) was troubled. God is giving the world dreams and their spirits are *"troubled"* over it. However, they still refuse to acknowledge God. Therefore, they go to palm readers, witches, diviners, psychics, etc to get the interpretation just like Pharaoh did. But *"no one could interpret"* the dreams they had. It was "un-interpretable." **Principle**: *When God gives a dream from Himself, none of the false ones in their* *wisdom can interpret it. It will require a true prophet with God's interpretation.*

The Living God is the only person who can interpret a dream given by Himself. It follows that if palm readers, psychics, witches and wizards can interpret a dream, that dream did not come from God. Do you understand? Only "The Prophet", Jesus, who is in us—can interpret a dream given by God. Therefore, if a palm reader, psychic, or diviners ever interpreted something for you and said, "God gave you that dream," it is a lie. God did not give you that dream, because when God gives a dream, only an apostle or prophet through the Spirit of Lord can interpret. Amen!

Genesis 41:15, NIV:
*Pharaoh said to Joseph, **"I had a dream, and no one can interpret it.** But I have heard it said of you that when you hear a dream you can interpret it."*

Genesis 41:16, NIV:
*"**I cannot do it,**" Joseph replied to Pharaoh, "but **God will give** Pharaoh the answer he desires."*

Joseph acknowledged that he could not interpret the dream, either, *"**but God** will give Pharaoh the answer he desires."* The Spirit of the Living God gives the interpretation **through** his apostles and prophets (Ephesians 3:5). In this age, interpretations will come through an apostle or prophet. One of the meanings of "apostle" is "sent one." Joseph who is a type of Jesus and a type of an apostle was *"sent"* to Egypt. *"And he* *sent* a man before them—Joseph, sold as a slave" (Psalm 105:17). The word *"sent"* is translated as *"apostello"* in the Septuagint—the Greek translation of the Hebrew Bible that Jesus and the early apostles used. *"Apostello"*, according to Vines Expository Dictionary, is **akin** to *"apostolos"* (an apostle); and according to Strong's Concordance *"apostolos"* is derived from *"apostello."* Therefore, Joseph foreshadowed the apostolic ministry of Jesus and apostles in general. God *"sent"* Joseph into Egypt, via slavery, to be an apostolic interpreter of the dreams of God (compare Philippians 2:7, NIV where "servant" means "slave"). The apostle's interpretation insured a better planning for the famine to come.

God's **mysteries** are revealed to His apostles and prophets, according to Ephesians 3:5-6 and Amos 3:7. For example, in Volume I, written in 1995, I discussed Islam being the greatest threat against America and the Church before September 11, 2001. In Volume II, written in 1998, I talked about the spirit of Greece and a tragedy happening in America before September 11, 2001. The problem is: The Church is not listening to the true prophets who know the interpretation of the future, which will enable preparation.

There is also apostolic directive for this generation, "The judgment" [in its many faces] will continue in America by God's **sovereignty.** It was **God** in His sovereignty who *"called for a famine upon the land"* in the days of Joseph (Psalm 105:16). About fourteen years ago, I was translated into the spirit (by providence); and God answered me in the secret place of thunder (Psalm 81:7).

I saw a huge eagle in flight, high in the clouds. The clouds were nimbus clouds. The color scheme of the eagle was as the flag of the United States of America. As I watched the eagle in majestic flight, with its large wings pushing through the nimbus clouds in the heights, I heard the sound of thunder. As I continued to listen, the sound of the thunder became a voice of thunder.

I heard the thundering in a gentle voice say, "Judgment, judgment, judgment..." As I heard this voice of thunder repeating itself with gentle peals, I saw myself on my face as I heard the secret of thunder; yet, I was on my knees. At that time I was young in the Lord and did not understand the vision (Daniel 7:27 last part).

Judgment came to Egypt; however, Joseph was in place to give an interpretation which preserved the peoples. Judgment is occurring; therefore, adjust your future accordingly as the Egyptians prepared for the famine. Learn to hear God's apostles and prophets. God reveals His secrets to them.

Ephesians 3:4-6, NIV:
[4] In reading this, then, you will be able to understand my insight into the mystery of Christ, [5] which was not made known to men in other generations as it has now been **revealed by (Gk.; in) the Spirit to God's holy apostles and prophets.** *[6] This mystery is that through the gospel the Gentiles are heirs together with Israel, members together of one body, and sharers together in the promise in Christ Jesus.*

Revelation 1:1, NIV:
The revelation of Jesus Christ, which God gave him to show his servants what must soon take place. ***He made it known by sending his angel to his servant John,***

Revelation 10:7, NIV:
But in the days when the seventh angel is about to sound his trumpet, the ***mystery of God*** *will be accomplished, just as he announced to his servants* ***the prophets.***

Amos 3:7, NIV:
Surely the Sovereign LORD ***does nothing without revealing his plan*** *to his servants the* ***prophets.***

In the Old Testament only Joseph, a sent one (an apostle), and Daniel, a prophet, could interpret the mysteries of God. Joseph and Daniel interpreted the mysterious dreams (Genesis 41: 25-32, Daniel 2). So like wise in this age, apostles and prophets will understand the mysteries of God. They will be able to interpret that which is **dreamed** and that which is **written.** Daniel had the ability to interpret dreams and things written (Daniel 1-2). Again, just as Joseph, an apostle of God was also able to define dreams that astrologers could not figure out; likewise God has apostles and prophets today who can define the times (Genesis 41; Daniel 2; Esther 1:13; I Chronicles 12:32).

Remember, when something is from the Lord Jesus, none of the false ones will be able to interpret it. They are limited like Jannes and Jambres. They could only perform three out of the ten miracles Moses demonstrated. So likewise, the false prophets can only interpret dreams from Satan. They are limited. They cannot understand or interpret the dream and writing of the Spirit of Jesus (I Corinthians 2:6-10). The reason is because the answer to God's visions and writing is too deep in God. Only God's sons and daughters are allowed in the deep things of God through the Holy Spirit (I Corinthians 2:9-10).

INTERPRETATION IS IN THE WOMB OF GOD

Daniel 2:17-18, NIV:
*[17] Then Daniel returned to his house and explained the matter to his friends Hananiah, Mishael and Azariah. [18] He urged them to plead for **mercy** from the God of heaven concerning this mystery, so that he and his friends might not be executed with the rest of the wise men of Babylon.*

Nebuchadnezzar had a dream and was troubled (Daniel 2:1). One of the reasons why this age is so troubled and seeking psychics and wizards is because God is speaking to them [Romans 10:18; Colossians 1:6 and 1:23]; but they like Nebuchadnezzar are forgetting. Nebuchadnezzar sent for the magicians, enchanters, astrologers and soothsayers to interpret the dream for him. The world is doing the same thing. However, as it was in Nebuchadnezzar's case, a prophet's interpretation was necessary.

They must tell him his own dream and they must interpret the dream with no information from the king.

The verdict for them if they could not do it was death (Daniel 2:2-11). Of course they could not, so the king ordered the false prophets execution (Daniel 2: 12-14). However, *"Daniel spoke with wisdom and tact"* (Daniel 2:14c). Daniel requested that an extension of time be granted to seek for the interpretation (Daniel 2:15-16). Daniel then went to his friends and urged them to pray for mercy from the God of heaven. It is from this statement I will show you some truth concerning the womb of God. Daniel *"urged them to plead for* **mercy** *from the God of heaven concerning this mystery"* dream (Daniel 2:18).

"Mercy," in the Hebrew is defined as **"womb as** *cherishing"* according to Strong's Concordance. This let us know that Daniel and his friends sought the **womb of God—His heart and Spirit.** The answer to every mystery is in the womb of God. False prophets are limited to what they can interpret, because they are not allowed in the womb of God. They are from the seed of Satan, and that which is satanic is destined for the lake of lightning and eternal fire (John 8:44; Matthews 25:41; Revelation 19:20). They cannot enter the womb of God unless they get saved. All true prophets must hear from the heart of God (Genesis 8: 21) and/or the womb of God to have the correct interpretation.

Daniel 2:19-20, NIV:

[19] **During the night the mystery was revealed to Daniel in a vision.** *Then Daniel praised the God of heaven* [20] *and said: "Praise be to the name of God for ever and ever;* **wisdom** *and power* **are his.**

Daniel heard the womb of God. The mystery was revealed to the prophet in a vision. This is filled with truth. **Principle**: *If something is unknown to you seek God's womb. He will reveal the mystery to you in the night seasons.* It will release worship in you. You will realize and say that *"wisdom and power are his."* Some of the many ways that God is using to reveal His secret to the world are the voice of dreams, visions and open vision (Genesis 41; Daniel 2; Daniel 4; Daniel 5). However, they are forgetting; because it comes as a language that only prophets and apostles can understand or interpret. People are seeking interpretation from the false ones; and they are not getting right answers. Therefore, they are full of rage and murder like Nebuchadnezzer.

The Church must go to the world and use the prophetic—Revelation 19:10c—as a **"tool"** to cause the Nebuchadnezzars of the world to worship God. Listen to what the king said after Daniel revealed the truth—*"The king said to Daniel, "Surely **your God** is **the God** of gods and **the Lord** of kings and **a revealer** of mysteries, for **you** were able to reveal this mystery"* (Daniel 2:47). The world, like Nebuchadnezzer, will acknowledge that Jesus is the God of gods, He is the Lord of kings as a result of prophetic understanding (compare I Corinthians 14:25). The Prophets interpretation will bring worship to God's sovereignty. Amen! People will worship the living God because *"**you** were able to reveal this mystery"* The key is: know that **only God** can give the interpretation as we seek his heart.

Genesis 8:21, NIV:
*The LORD smelled the pleasing aroma and **said in his*** ***heart:** "Never again will I curse the ground because of man, even though every inclination of his heart is evil from childhood. And never again will I destroy all living creatures, as I have done.*

The key to **hearing** is to seek the Lord by using *"all kinds of prayer and requests,"* in the Spirit (Ephesians 6:18). The Father, in His sovereign timing, will allow us to hear the heart of God. We are able to understand that God reversed a curse because Noah, a man with like passion like us, was able to hear the **heart** of God. Before Noah heard God's heart, he built an altar. One of the symbols of the altar is prayer.

Genesis 8:20, NIV:
*Then Noah **built an altar to the LORD** and, taking some of all the clean animals and clean birds, he sacrificed burnt offerings on it.*

After the flood of judgment, Noah *"built an altar to the LORD."* He built prayer and it *"smelled sweet"* to God. The bible says that prayer is as sweet incense (Psalm 141:2; Revelation 8:1-5). This incense is the sweet smell of prayer that ascends into God's nose.

Revelation 5:8, NIV:
*And when he had taken it, the four living creatures and the twenty-four elders fell down before the Lamb. Each one had a harp and they were holding **golden bowls full of incense**, which are the **prayers** of the saints.*

Prayers are incense. The altar that Noah built was a type of prayer to God. He offered *"burnt offerings"* on this altar. The Hebrew word for *burnt offerings* means *"a step as ascending"* (Strong's # 5930). The root word for burnt offerings means to *"ascend."* This shows us that we must ascend in prayer. Noah's offering of prayer ascended to God and, it was sweet like incense to God. The result was: God allowed Noah to hear His **heart.**

Genesis 8:21, NIV:
*The LORD smelled the pleasing aroma and **said** in his **heart:** "Never again will I curse the ground because of man, even though every inclination of his heart is evil from childhood. And never again will I destroy all living creatures, as I have done."*

Did you hear what I heard? **Noah heard the heart of God.** *"The LORD ... **said** in his **heart.**"* If he did not hear God's heart, the writer could not have recorded what we just read in the verse above. Noah heard God's heart. God spoke in His own heart and reversed a curse on the earth. This is significant. There are things that will never be heard until we build a lifestyle dependent on prayer to the living God. We must build an altar of persistent prayer in our home. The secrets of God are revealed from His heart and womb.

We must "ascend" in prayer like the burnt offerings; and as we ascend in the Spirit, we will understand the mysteries of God (II Corinthians 12). Men ruled by Babel, like Belshazzar, cannot understand the writings of God, especially, the handwritings of judgment (Daniel 5). Men of prayer who seek the womb of God, they can understand. Daniel exemplified this fully. He had developed a prayer life of three times a day: *"Three times a day he got down on his knees and prayed, giving thanks to his God"* (Daniel 6:10)

Daniel must have learned from the first experience that the womb or heart of God is the way to interpreting. This dedication led to the interpreting the final judgment on Babylon. It is the apostles and prophets who are declaring the fall of Babylon by interpreting the book of Revelation, Zechariah, Daniel, etc.

THE INSCRIPTION OF JUDGMENT

Daniel 5:5-6, NIV:
[5] *Suddenly the fingers of a human hand appeared and **wrote** on the plaster of the wall, near the **lampstand** in the royal palace. The king watched the hand as it wrote.*
[6] *His face turned pale and he was so **frightened** that his knees knocked together and his legs gave way.*

Belshazzar was having a party with drinking wine (symbolic of blood, Revelation 17:6) from the goblets of the temple of God (Daniel 5:1-4 with I Corinthians 3:16). This was an offence to God. Therefore, God sent the writing of judgment. *"**Suddenly** the fingers of a human hand appeared and **wrote** on the plaster of the wall, near the lampstand in the royal palace"* (Daniel 5: 5). This caused a panic in the king and his men. He did the same thing Pharaoh, Nebuchadnezzer and the children of this age do. *"The king called out for the enchanters, astrologers and diviners"* (Daniel 5:7). This action by the king was in vain.

The false prophets of Babylon are limited. They are fakes. Listen to the scripture: *"Then all the king's wise men came in, **but they could not read the writing or tell the king what it meant"*** (Daniel 5:8). The reason why they could not was because they were not of God. They do not have the Spirit of God (I Corinthians 2:10). Remember I said earlier, when a word, vision, dream, directions, etc is from God, no astrology reading, no palm reading, no psychic reading, no wizards, or no diviners can interpret it.

Therefore, if these kinds of people are reading for you, whatever they say is not from God. Why? They **cannot** *"read the writing"* from God. The only thing they can understand is that which is from demons. The scripture calls it doctrines, teachings, of devils (I Timothy 4:1). Things are going to get *"**frightening"*** for the world when their interpreters fail. They will have no choice but to turn to the Living God. His name is Jesus, King of kings and Lord of lords. He is blessed forever more. The mother queen advised: *"**Call for Daniel, and**

he will tell *you what the writing means"* (Daniel 5:12, last part).

True apostles and prophets must be called to give understanding concerning the mystery of Babel's Judgment (Revelation 16:19-17:1 with Daniel 5:12). The angel gave the apostle John the revelation of judgment of the great prostitute—Mystery Babylon (Revelation 17:1-5). The Spirit of God gave Daniel the interpretation of the writing concerning Babylon of his time. *Principle*: *It will be the apostolic and prophetic team that will understand and interpret the mystery of judgment against Mystery Babylon.* Those who walk in the Spirit will interpret the writing of God (Galatians 5:25, I Corinthians 2:14-16).

IN THE SPIRIT OF GOD

Revelation 1:10-11, NIV:
[10] *On the Lord's Day I **was** in **the Spirit,** and I heard behind me a loud voice like a trumpet,* [11] *which said: "Write on a scroll what you see and send it to the seven churches: to Ephesus, Smyrna, Pergamum, Thyatira, Sardis, Philadelphia and Laodicea."*

Let us take a look at the Lamb's interpretation, which can only be received in the Spirit. John *"was in the Spirit"* on the Lord's Day. On **the Lord's Day** (not Sunday as supposed by some), John *"was"* in the Spirit. The word *"was"* is the Greek word *"ginomai"* and is defined as *"a prolongation and middle voice form of a primary verb; to cause to be ("gen"-erate), i.e.*

(reflexively) to become (come into being), used with great latitude (literal, figurative, intensive, etc.):" [Strong's # 1096]. It is translated ***"born"*** in the New International Version.

Galatians 4:4, NIV:
*But when the time had fully come, God sent his Son, **born** of a woman, born under law...*

The point is this: John was ***birthed*** into the Spirit realm. He ***"became"*** in the Spirit. He was ***"caused to be"*** in the Spirit. Therefore, the writings of Revelation are ***spirit***ual. It can only be interpreted by those **in** the Spirit God. I will say like Paul, *"⁴ In reading this, then, you will be able to understand my insight into the mystery of Christ, ⁵ which was not made known to men in other generations as it has now been revealed **by the Spirit (lit.; in the Spirit)** to God's holy apostles and prophets"* (Ephesians 3:4-5, NIV).

Those *"born"* from above can *"see the kingdom of God"* (John 3:3). John was invited to go up to heaven, because Jesus wanted to *"show"* him some things that will take place (Revelation 4:1). The scripture said, *"At once I was in the Spirit."*

Revelation 4:1-2, NIV:
*¹ After this I looked, and there before me was a door standing open in heaven. And the voice I had first heard speaking to me like a trumpet said, "Come up here, and I will show you what must take place after this." ²**At once***

I was in the Spirit, and there before me was a throne in heaven with someone sitting on it.

Did you catch that or is your eyes blinded? I will show you the truth. He was invited to heaven, and **at once** he was in the Spirit. *Thus, Heaven is in the Spirit.* Heaven is not millions of miles away. Heaven is right next to you. Paul said to **"walk in the Spirit"** (Galatians 5:16 and 5:25). Walking in the Spirit has to do with the mind. Revelation 4:1-2 lets us know that heaven is in the Spirit. Therefore, when we walk in the spirit we are walking in heaven. When we walk in the Spirit, or we are birthed in the Spirit; we can *"see"* heaven. Yes! Yes! Yes!

It was after John was birthed into the Spirit that he was able to see the Lamb of God open the book of Revelation to him. The book was sealed. God gave it to Jesus (Revelation 1:1) Jesus gave it to John at God's choosing. And God did all this through His Spirit (Revelation 4:2).

I Corinthians 2:9-10, NIV:
[9] *However, as it is written: "No eye has seen, no ear has heard, no mind has conceived what God has prepared for those who love him" –* [10] **but God has revealed it to us by his Spirit.** *The Spirit searches all things, even the deep things of God.*

Revelation 4:2, NIV:
*At once **I was in the Spirit,** and there before me was a throne in heaven with someone sitting on it.*

Revelation 5:1-5, NIV:
*¹ Then I saw in the right hand of him who sat on the throne a scroll with writing on both sides and sealed with seven seals. ² And I saw a mighty angel proclaiming in a loud voice, "Who is worthy to break the seals and open the scroll?" ³ But no one in heaven or on earth or under the earth could open the scroll or even look inside it. ⁴ I wept and wept because **no one** was found who was worthy to open the scroll or look inside. ⁵ Then one of the elders said to me, "Do not weep! See, the **Lion of the tribe of Judah,** the Root of David, has triumphed. **He** is able to open the scroll and its seven seals."*

It was in the Spirit that John saw the scroll sealed with seven seals. No one was found worthy to open the scroll or look inside. There are some things that are seen by the populous, yet the understanding is sealed by God. Nebuchadnezzar, Belshazzar and Pharaoh experienced this first hand. However, those who are spiritual and elected by God's graceful Lamb will be allowed to see, know again, interpret and understand that which was once unlawful to utter (II Corinthians 12:4).

The "elect", the Church, of the Lamb of God will be able to understand mysteries that was once hidden (Revelation 5:5, Colossians 1:25-26, Ephesians 3: 1-5) **through** His holy apostles and prophets. Everything apostles and prophets receive is for the body. Listen to the language of Paul again: *"² Surely you have heard* *about the administration of God's grace **that was given to me for you,*** [3] *that is, the mystery made known to me by revelation, as I have already written briefly"* (Ephesians 3:2-3, NIV).

The Lamb of God is continually opening the writings of truth through the apostles and prophets for the Church. Jesus will then interpret through the Church the dreams/writings that the world (Egypt and Babylon) cannot understand (Daniel 5, Genesis 41, Acts 8:25-39). John said, *"I watched as **the Lamb opened** the first of the seven seals"* (Revelation 6:1a).

It was the Lamb who opened all of the seals on the scroll. Jesus is revealing himself to His apostles and prophets. The purpose is to make known his death, burial and resurrection to those who need it. I reiterate, the Revelation of Jesus will be made know to His apostles and prophets (Revelation1:1). The false ones of the world are blinded to the dream, and writings of God (Daniel 2; Daniel 5, Genesis 41).

It will take Jesus being revealed in the right way to interpret the dreams and visions that cannot be interpreted by the false prophets of the world. The limited power of the many false prophets will be exposed. God is exposing all the false ones through His Word. Remember according to Hebrews 4:12-13, the Word of God is the eyes of God. Do not partake with antichrists—spirits or people. Instead, ask God to show you all that he wants you to have in the Christ—Jesus. Rely on Jesus' righteousness; develop prayer, develop fasting and a good study habits in your life. Make sure that you follow the voice of His leaders.

Finally, my brothers, walk in the Spirit of Jesus, seek the womb of God and do not fulfill the lust of this sinful generation. Seek the Lord Jesus and abstain from the false ones. They may "war" against us but remember, *"...The Lamb will overcome them because **he is** Lord of lord and King of kings—**and with him** will be his called, chosen and **faithful followers"** (Revelation 17:14). Be faithful to the Lord. The grace of the Lord Jesus fills your heart. Amen!

Other Books

Sexual Healing, By Judith Peart: <u>FOREWORD:</u> "Your hearts will be touched, your feelings, and emotions challenged as you read this book of truth and love. Judith, out of a heart of love has shed light on the deception, and bondages of past sins in our lives, as an example of the healing power and love of our heavenly Father; as we too yield to the spirit of God, we too can take courage to be healed, delivered and set free. Thank you Judith for your courage and transparency to help others as the Holy Spirit has helped you. Freely you have received. Freely you have given." (Dr. Sandra Phillips Hayden, Word Alive! Worship Center, Baltimore, MD)

The False Prophet, Alias, Another Beast, Volume I of III, By Donald Peart: <u>THE FALSE PROPHET, ALIAS, ANOTHER BEAST</u> is a comprehensive study manual that exposes "ANOTHER BEAST", and his purpose, behind the many false teachings of our day. Some of these doctrines of devils include: psychic, new age, Islam, satanic worship, the lie of homosexuality, and what is the mark of the beast.

The Beast, Volume II of III, By Donald Peart: <u>THE BEAST</u> is a broad look at the so called antichrist. It is a subject that has caused fear in so many with respect to the future. However, as one will see, the beast and his mark are not only future, but the beast and his mark is a present reality. This book explores history, culture and most importantly The Book to demonstrate the reality of the beast presently and in times to come. REMEMBER HISTORY REPEATS ITSELF.

The Shepherd's Tent
P.O. Box 1041
Randallstown, MD 21133